CHANGE YOURSELF

CHRISTINA L. MARTINI AND DAVID G. SUSLER

Part of the Paradigm Shift Series

CHANGE YOURSELF

ISBN 978-1-961185-78-4 (Paperback)
ISBN 978-1-961185-80-7 (Hardcover)
ISBN 978-1-961185-81-4 (eBook)

Cover Design, Book Formatting & Layout by *in omnia paratus publishing llc*

www.inomniaparatuspublishing.com

We are forever grateful to so many people for the professionals and individuals we are today. None of this would have been possible without the love, support, coaching and advice that we have received over the years.

We dedicate *Change Yourself* to our family, friends, colleagues, clients, mentors, coaches, confidantes, professors, teachers, role models and others who have so generously touched our lives and left their indelible imprints on us.

You know who you are.

Wishing you all the best, Howard!

Table of Contents

Preface 1

Getting Personal 5

Law School 9

Recruiting and Retention: A Shared Responsibility 13

Words of Wisdom for New and Experienced Lawyers 23

Comparing and Contrasting: In-House vs. Private Practice 33

Client Service: The Key to Success 53

Professional Development 79

Mentoring and Executive Coaching 89

Your Personal Brand 97

Emotional Intelligence: The Key to Stronger Leadership,
Resilience and Connection 103

Quiet Strength: The Power of Introverts 113

Going Global 119

Leadership 121

Success is Never a One-Person Show 127

Wellness is a Leadership Tool, Not a Luxury 131

Navigating Uncertainty 137

Role Models, Confidantes and the Power of Mutual Trust 145

Pro Bono, Volunteering and Extracurriculars 151

Resolutions and Goal Setting 161

Innovation, Technology and Artificial Intelligence: Growth in
Motion 171

Skills of a Great Professional 179

Leaving a Legacy 221

Recommended Reading List 227

Additional Resources 229

Notes... 231

PREFACE

Nothing happens until something moves.
- Albert Einstein

A paradigm shift is defined as a fundamental change in how we think about or do something that leads to a new and different understanding or approach to a situation. This change often involves a significant shift in our beliefs, practices and perspectives, and can be inspired by the introduction of new knowledge or evidence.

As a practicing attorney with over 30 years of professional experience in BigLaw across a wide variety of practice areas, I have had countless opportunities to work with a wide range of clients on bet the company legal matters. These experiences inspired me over two decades ago to start sharing my professional and personal insights through various thought leadership, including my podcast (aptly named Paradigm Shift), as well as through dozens of columns, many written in tandem with my husband, who is also a lawyer and brings his own perspective and professional experiences.

This year, as I considered the many topics I have written about for over 20 years, I quickly realized that most, if not all, of them carry even more value now than at the time I had originally written about them, not only for my fellow legal professionals for whom they were originally written, but for everyone else. And, just like that, the idea for this book and our other book, *Change Your Business*, was born. Both books are intended to complement one another, and while they each have some of the same content, *Change Yourself* is focused on individuals and *Change Your Business* is targeted to organizations.

As I reflect on my legal career, and the professional and personal life I have created, I feel nothing short of blessed – blessed to have the family, friends, clients and colleagues, without whom none of this would have been possible, and blessed for the serendipities and opportunities which have crossed my path and transformed my journey of incredibly hard work and dedication to one which has been even more fulfilling and meaningful than I could have ever imagined. I firmly believe in the notion of paying it forward, and my hope is that as you read this book, you are better for having done so and that there is at least one takeaway for you that is insightful and transformative.

I wish you all the best on your professional and personal path, and in experiencing your own paradigm shift.

Christina L. Martini

I grew up in Decatur, Illinois, surrounded by lawyers - my father, my oldest sister, two great uncles, many other relatives, all lawyers. Dinner time discussions in my family often centered around my father giving us factual scenarios based on his cases (no names, despite my always asking). Ultimately, those discussions were lessons in critical thinking and analysis, ethics and morals. I looked forward to those discussions, and they were the seeds, planted at an early age, of my desire to follow in my father's footsteps and pursue a career as a plaintiff's personal injury lawyer.

Fast forward a number of years, I graduated from law school and started my career as a personal injury lawyer, first on the defense side, then switching to the plaintiff side six years later. I finally achieved my life's goal. But a funny thing happened on the way to achieving my dream - a couple of years into being a plaintiff's PI attorney, I realized I actually did not enjoy it. I was burned out and knew I could not do that forever. The problem was that I had no Plan B.

After a lot of soul-searching and networking, I decided to try becoming an in-house lawyer. I landed my first in-house job and, with a huge leap of faith, I embarked on an amazing journey that continues to this day. As of this writing, with over 26 years as an in-house generalist, I am still learning, still growing as a lawyer and as a person, and I still love what I do. With that 180° shift in focus, and re-engineering my career from personal injury litigation to in-house business generalist, I not only found a way to practice law that I enjoy, I found a way to fulfill my larger purpose: to help improve the lives of my clients and of those I work with in ways that feel genuinely aligned with who I am and what I always wanted to accomplish as a lawyer and in this world.

One of the primary lessons I learned along this journey is that I developed a comfort zone in being outside of my comfort zone. We learn the most from those situations where we face adversity, challenging the ideas and narratives we assume to be true. In such situations and experiences, we are able to test what we are made of and experience monumental paradigm shifts in our lives, relationships and careers.

David G. Susler

Getting Personal

Having two lawyers in one household is more of a blessing than a curse. Scheduling tends to be the biggest challenge we face, particularly when we both have meetings into the evening or need to be on the road at the same time. When that happens, we need to figure out how we are going to take care of our pets and other household responsibilities. At those times, it is also challenging to connect with each other to see how the other is doing and to catch up on the events of the day, especially if there is a significant time zone disparity. That can be tough, especially when schedules are intense over a longer period of time. That being said, there are very few people who can truly understand both the rewards and challenges of being a lawyer as well as another lawyer can, and one cannot underestimate the importance of being with someone who really gets it. For us, this is how it has always been, so it never occurred to either of us as something unusual or difficult.

From Christina's perspective:

"I grew up in Highland Park, a suburb of Chicago. I am the 3rd of four children and the only girl. I am blessed to have a wonderful family of extremely intelligent, talented, down to earth individuals who have been a great source of inspiration to me. We all have science backgrounds, and as I attended engineering school, I drew a lot of support from them. It was not easy being one of very few women in engineering more than 30 years ago.

When I was a senior in high school, my mother passed away suddenly. I was very close to her and her death was devastating and completely changed my life going forward. From that moment, I was forced to be independent and self-sufficient. I also felt responsible for making a positive difference in the world and for making my family proud. My mom was Latina and aspired to be a doctor. She was brilliant and most certainly capable, but part of a generation which made it very difficult for her to fulfill her dream. As the next generation, I feel it is my responsibility to help break down those barriers.

I received my Undergraduate Degree in Industrial Engineering. While in college, I started my Master's Degree, also in Industrial Engineering, and had been offered a full scholarship to pursue a PhD. I put both on hold once I was accepted into Northwestern School of Law. I started law school in 1991, and I enrolled because I was intellectually curious about the law. Up until that point, all of my academic and work experiences had been focused on the sciences and engineering, and I felt drawn to this other world of precise communication with words rather than with numbers. I have always loved to read and write, and engineering does not afford many opportunities to do that, so that excited me about the law as well. If I could do it all over again, I would have found a way to finish my Master's and gotten my PhD in addition to my Law Degree.

I often reflect on the tremendous education and skillset I developed as an engineer and the amazing asset it has been for my practice and development as a professional. Like the law, engineering teaches you how to think and reason. It also develops you into a critical thinker who problem solves and processes issues in a very different way from other disciplines. Process engineering, which is much of what manufacturing is, provides skills which are readily applicable across all different facets of legal practice as well as in the management and operations aspects of the business side of the law.

Being the best professional and person I can be inspires me to get up each morning. My compass is directed at making as much of a positive difference for my clients and the community as possible. My family is a tremendous inspiration - my father and three brothers in particular, who have shown extraordinary strength and perseverance in the face of overwhelming adversity and loss and whose professional and personal successes are awe-inspiring. Although she died nearly 40 years ago, my mother continues to inspire me every day. She was so ahead of her time in her brilliance, courage and tenacity to be so much more than just another Mexican immigrant victimized by discrimination and prejudice. David inspires me every day with his generosity, patience, compassion and support. My friends, colleagues and mentors inspire me to be the best I can be, to see issues from multiple angles and to pay it forward by helping the younger generations along."

From David's perspective:

"I grew up in Decatur, a city in central Illinois which then had about 95,000 people. To choose one thing of greatest impact in my life is difficult but I have to say our family dinner conversations as I was growing up played a key role. My father was a lawyer and we often discussed his cases. This was not merely my dad telling stories. He presented various factual scenarios to elicit discussion and along the way taught such life tools as logic, ethics and the importance of making a positive difference in the world. Those were always my favorite conversations and a large part of the foundation of why I became a lawyer.

I decided as a young child that I wanted to be a lawyer. Building on our family dinner time conversations, as well as the general principles I learned from my parents and my religion, I knew I wanted to help people and to make a difference. The law seemed to be the best vehicle by which to accomplish those goals.

When asked if there is anything I would change, on one hand my answer is nothing, because the career I have had makes me the lawyer I am today, and I currently have a job and career that I love. However, had I known then what I know now, I would have taken more business and finance courses in college. I would still have done personal-injury work but maybe would have done commercial litigation earlier. Also, had I realized then how valuable and fun being active in bar associations is, I would have been active from the outset of my career, instead of waiting until 15 years into it.

I have had the honor and privilege of mentoring hundreds of law students and Posse scholars over the past 20 years. They are all amazing, intelligent, driven leaders, on the cusp of their careers, and I leave every interaction with them inspired. My family has also always inspired me, especially my father and great uncles, all of whom were lawyers. They passed on to me a love for the law and respect for the profession and I constantly aspire to honor their names and reputations. A constant in my life for nearly 30 years that I can always rely on is my wife. Her inexorable drive towards excellence, for continuous improvement both professionally and personally, is eminently inspiring to me. The fantastic career I have today is, in large part, due to the inspiration I draw from her."

Law School

Does it Matter Where You Go to School?

Where you go to law school can be very important depending on what your end game is. If you decide you just want to get a legal education, and you do not plan to practice, this decision may not matter as much. But if you are looking to maximize job prospects, as well as your income potential, the choice of law school can matter greatly. This is particularly true if you are graduating into a tough economy. If you do not have work experience and are looking for a job, where you went to law school is going to be a critical factor - especially if you want to go into BigLaw. Christina explains, *"When I was the hiring partner of my firm, I tried to take a more holistic approach toward candidates. The law school you attend is important, but as a hiring committee we try to look at other factors, such as work experience, life experience, academic credentials, emotional intelligence and how folks came across in interviews."*

You need to ask yourself, *"Do I want to practice at a small firm? Do I want to practice in a small city? Do I want to practice in government or go into academia? Do I even want to practice law?"* Some people use their law school education to rise up through the ranks in business. While your law school is important in getting your first job, once you graduate law school, pass the bar exam, and become a practicing lawyer, your law school is not as dispositive on how good of a lawyer you are and can become. Ultimately, it does not determine whether you will have a successful, satisfying legal career.

Furthermore, what you did during your time in law school can be important. You should take as broad a range of courses as you can, and take courses that you find interesting, but which may not be in your chosen practice area. Ultimately, a more holistic professional with a well-rounded education is far more important than where you went to law school.

Advice for Prospective Law School Students

The legal profession has undergone dramatic transformation in recent history. As the rules of the game continue to evolve, it is important for students to understand and accept this perpetual state of change before investing significant time and money in a law school education. There is a level of determination, maturity, business savvy and sophistication that is essential for future generations of lawyers. We recommend that law students actively seek ways to ensure they are effectively positioning themselves for success and to be very clear about what they hope to accomplish with a Law Degree, before going to law school. Taking time to gain work experience between college and law school is one way to ensure that a career in the law is what you really want.

Law students must also temper their expectations regarding job prospects during and especially after school. Students need to start their job search almost immediately after starting school. That does not necessarily mean applying for jobs right away, but rather building the foundation needed to be able to find a job when appropriate. That means networking - go to law firm and bar association programs and events, and meet lawyers while there. Do not solely rely on OCI (on-campus interviewing) for summer or permanent jobs. Consider other job options - for example, smaller firms, not-for-profit organizations, and government agencies.

Although starting in-house straight from law school is rare, the interest in practicing in-house as a career goal has increased considerably in recent years, as have the number of in-house summer internships. Such programs are a good introduction to in-house practice, provide hands-on practical experience and experience working inside a corporation rather than a law firm. They can also provide excellent networking opportunities.

Summer associate programs are generally more conservative and more focused on specific practice group needs and on ensuring the summer associate is a good long-term fit with the firm. These programs are not as much about entertainment and selling the summer associate on the firm as they have been in the past. Since all businesses are trying to do more with less, these programs are often leaner, more focused and more competitive than they were when we started our careers. Some firms have made the decision that summer programs no longer align with their workforce needs and have decided to phase them out completely. As this phenomenon continues, law students will be forced to be more creative and strategic in finding ways to get the experience they need both before and upon graduation.

While pure legal knowledge is important, both substantively as well as practically - knowing the law and how it applies - success is also driven by emotional intelligence, fire in the belly, passion for what you do, and passion for life, because these qualities translate into success and fulfillment in the profession.

Our Most Valuable Lessons from Law School

From Christina's perspective:

"There are a few important lessons I learned. Law school in many ways is like learning a foreign language, and practicing law is much the same experience - developing your stamina and learning by immersion. To be a strong performer in any endeavor, you need to jump in headfirst, focus, and relentlessly work toward your goal. Law school also teaches rigor to one's thought process and problem-solving, much like engineering school did for me. It is an invaluable tool, not just in the practice of law but in life. I also learned that every issue has more than one answer or legitimate point of view. This is important, not only in advocating for clients but also when approaching leadership and decision-making, both within and outside the law."

From David's perspective:

"This is tough because my focus in law school was so different than it is today. I planned on being a personal injury attorney and there were few courses directly relevant to such a career beyond torts, evidence and trial advocacy. When I went in-house, my focus shifted to a commercial business practice. Beyond the core courses generally taught in the 1L year, I think intellectual property, bankruptcy, evidence and trial advocacy remain among the most valuable courses for my career."

The Future of Law School

We hope that law school curricula will continue to evolve and not only teach the skills required to be a successful lawyer but also to sensitize students and enable them to hone their skills. Defining those skills and integrating them into law school curricula is important. Law schools should consider taking the last year of school and making it into a clinic year with on-the-job experience, pushing students outside of the classroom and into the real world to get the experience they need and to help them understand what a service, client-driven business looks like. It takes a lot of time to develop the skills necessary to be an effective legal advisor and counselor, so the sooner law students begin thinking that way the better. Law schools should continue to look at admissions policies and whether having students work for a year or two between college and law school will help their student body gain a certain maturity and understanding that they do not get only as a student.

Recruiting and Retention: A Shared Responsibility

Recruiting and retaining talent is one of an organization's most complex and critical challenges. It requires a thoughtful, strategic approach that acknowledges talent management's nuanced, evolving nature. Whether you are on the hiring or candidate side, there is a shared responsibility for making the process productive, meaningful and sustainable.

The Foundations of Talent Management

Talent management is much more than filling seats or posting job openings. It begins with a thorough and honest understanding of your needs and goals, while also being self-aware and honest about your business' strengths and weaknesses. Once you have identified what success looks like for a particular role and for the organization as a whole, you must find and develop people who align with that vision.

Developing talent extends well beyond formal industry training. While substantive, technical skills are essential, soft skills are equally important and are often inextricably linked to emotional intelligence and client service orientation. These "intangibles" frequently determine whether someone will thrive in the culture, and whether they will merely meet or exceed client expectations.

Effective talent management also means ensuring that individuals complement one another, so the strengths of some offset the weaknesses of others. Leadership development and succession planning are crucial to this process, with the need to look at business objectives holistically and assess whether your workforce's skillsets meaningfully align with those objectives.

From Hiring to Development: A Continuum

Hiring the right people is only the first step in the process. Once onboard, ongoing development and training are critical to their success and retention. This means setting clear goals, providing honest, constructive feedback, and proactive career planning. Talent management also requires real-time cooperation and alignment between business strategy and human resources.

This approach helps ensure that you have the right people not only for today's needs but also for the long term. The business world is not static; people grow and change over time. You need to anticipate and support that growth, guiding employees along trajectories that benefit both their careers and the organization's evolving demands. People develop in different ways, and it is important to discern how best to harness each individual's potential, using what you know works well and adapting where it doesn't. Without strong talent management, organizations risk stagnation, talent drain and missed opportunities for growth. Failing to provide the necessary resources, training and growth opportunities, or not giving employees a stake in the organization's success, can often lead to unnecessary turnover. Talent management applies to all employees, not just top performers. Every organization needs leaders and support staff. Neglecting any group can lead to significant organizational decline.

The Cost of Turnover and the Value of Care

Losing valuable employees is not just disruptive - it is also costly in terms of knowledge drain, time and financial impact. It costs far more to replace an employee than to properly train and develop existing ones. If you take care of your employees, they will take care of you and your business.

This mindset fosters loyalty, motivation and a culture where people are empowered to do their best work.

No hiring process can fully guarantee long-term success. Some people shine early on, but are not able to sustain it. Others may not seem like the perfect fit initially, but grow into rock stars with the right amount of support. Not every employee will be right for every organization forever, and that is okay. Meaningful contributions can happen no matter what the tenure, and some employees ultimately find greater success elsewhere. Against this backdrop, it is important to maintain realistic expectations and embrace talent mobility as part of the organizational life cycle.

The Importance of Delegation and Talent Leveraging

Leaders must be willing to meaningfully delegate. The people we hire need opportunities to take on responsibilities, both routine and challenging, to fully develop their skills. It is also essential in building well–leveraged teams to handle the work. Indeed, clients expect having the lowest-cost providers doing the work, and this frees up more senior team members to work on important, high–value tasks that only they can do. Staying attuned to how best to spot and develop talent within our organization and industry is essential. This means analyzing who is succeeding and why, then institutionalizing the practices contributing to that success. Developing talent takes time and commitment, but if done correctly, it can become a competitive advantage.

Hiring Right: Beyond Resumes and Charm

When hiring, it is essential that you clearly identify your team's needs and hire candidates with the right qualifications. Being bright or personable alone does not guarantee a good fit.

Our collective experience has taught us that effective recruiting hinges on asking the right questions. If you feel lukewarm about a candidate, it usually means you should not extend an offer. Evaluating candidates based on how they handle interviews under pressure is just as important as what is on their resumes. Trust your intuition: if something doesn't add up, explore it further, and if the answer remains unsatisfactory, the candidate is not likely a good fit.

Interviewing from Both Sides

Candidates must prepare thoroughly for interviews. Research the organization thoroughly: review public information, speak with current employees, and research with whom you are interviewing. This preparation helps confirm whether the organization and role align with your short- and long-term goals, and demonstrates your genuine interest in the position, setting you apart from other candidates. If you realize during the interview process that a role is not a good fit, be honest with yourself and the potential employer. A positive, realistic approach serves everyone's best interests.

Be yourself. Do not try to guess what the interviewer wants to hear; they will see through it. Ask thoughtful questions. Sometimes, the quality of your questions is the tipping point between equally qualified candidates. Chase what truly interests you, not just what seems like the easiest or most prestigious option.

For the employers out there, it is imperative that you have the right people conduct interviews. They are the face of your organization and must exercise discernment and good judgment. They also need to be friendly, respectful and diplomatic. A consensus on what constitutes a successful hire can help avoid "freestyle interviewing," where decisions are made based on likeability rather than fit. Looking back at past hires can provide valuable insights for moving forward. Identifying common traits in successful employees can help create a predictive index to guide future recruiting efforts.

Beyond Traditional Metrics: Innovating Talent Identification

Michael Lewis' groundbreaking bestseller, *Moneyball,* chronicled the scouting method developed by the Oakland A's General Manager, Billy Beane, that revolutionized how baseball scouts evaluate talent, and its lessons apply to recruiting professionals as well. As in baseball, talent in business is not always apparent at first glance. Just as a player might be more valuable as a pinch hitter than a starter, a professional's actual value emerges in context, through how they align with clients, strategies and team dynamics.

We need to regularly revisit how we define talent and success. Traditional metrics may no longer suffice. As the business world continues to rapidly evolve, we must question whether our long-held assumptions about qualifications, experience and productivity remain valid. In our experience, success depends less on initial promise and more on sustained performance, and on how well we harness strengths and support development over time. We must find individuals capable, committed and open to mentoring, growth and change.

Aligning Talent and Business Needs Over Time

As markets and organizational lifecycles evolve, so do our workforce needs. We must forecast these changes realistically and set clear expectations for how long members of our workforce have to demonstrate value, and to define what success needs to look like.

Just like baseball players get traded or leave as free agents, professionals will often move on to organizations better suited to their skills during particular stages of their careers. Employee mobility is a natural and fundamental part of a healthy recruiting cycle. Recruiting is both an investment in our future, as well as the legacy we leave behind.

Internships: Advice For Success

Internships remain a vital recruitment tool for many organizations. Whether you are applying for or managing internship programs, we have several key insights that can help maximize success:

1. **View the internship as one long interview.** One of the biggest mistakes that summer interns make is believing they have locked in a permanent offer once they land their summer internship. However, many organizations hire more summer interns than they will ultimately need as full-time employees, so their summer program is actually a competition for spots. Moreover, even if you are at a business where there is space for everyone who is hired into the summer program, if you fall short of expectations, you may not get an offer. Therefore, it is imperative that you conduct yourself professionally and do your best at all times.

2. **Take the work seriously.** Summer internships are designed to give students a sense of what it is like to be a full-time member of an organization. It is a mix of work and social activities. Depending on the business, it can seem like a full-time job just to keep up with all the fun. Remember that you need to do a great job on all of your assignments and make sure that you are completing a sufficient number of assignments of the type needed to fully demonstrate and evaluate your capabilities.

3. **Get to know your fellow interns.** Many of us are in relationship-driven businesses. You should make sure you develop strong ties with your fellow summer interns. If all goes well and you receive an offer, you will be working

alongside them after graduation. They can be a great source of often-needed peer guidance and support, particularly during the more challenging times in your career.

4. **Get to know the organization's permanent employees and staff.** The bedrock of every organization is its people. Just as it is important for you to get to know your fellow summer interns, it is equally imperative to develop relationships with the organization's permanent employees and staff. They will be invaluable in helping you learn how to succeed and get things done. You need to have allies who are invested in your success.

5. **Observe the Golden Rule.** It sounds so simple, but it can prove challenging. Demonstrating respect for others is the cornerstone to showing that you have the requisite emotional intelligence to fit within the fabric of the organization. You must do more than just prove that you can do the work - you need to show that you are collaborative, collegial and able to get along with others.

6. **Learn to juggle.** Multitasking is a part of everyday life, especially as a professional. Summer programs are designed to force participants to develop and hone their time management skills and to demonstrate that they can effectively juggle all of the different responsibilities that come with being a successful employee. Be careful about saying "no" to any of the various work and social activities presented to you during the summer.

7. **Find your people.** Being a summer intern can sometimes feel overwhelming, especially as you are starting out and trying to get to know everyone. Be sure to set aside time

every day to walk the halls, and find individuals with whom you meaningfully connect and focus on developing those relationships. It is often by meeting people organically that the best mentoring happens.

8. **Actively seek out feedback.** The best internship programs are designed to provide frequent, comprehensive and honest feedback. Beyond whatever formal tools there may be, take the opportunity to speak directly with those giving you assignments and those who are running the program to hear their comments firsthand and take their suggestions to heart. The information they provide will be helpful, and you will be seen as engaged and proactive about your career.

9. **Learn from your mistakes.** We all make mistakes, and no one is perfect. What is important is that we learn from them. When something does not go as planned, you should take a step back, figure out what happened and how to do it better the next time, and then be sure to adjust your approach accordingly.

10. **Is this the right place for me?** Many organizations have a rigorous interview process before deciding who to hire into their summer programs. The hope is that by the end of the summer, the intern's performance has in large part validated these choices. That being said, it sometimes becomes clear over the course of the summer that certain people may not be a good long-term fit. These decisions should be a two-way street, meaning that both the organization and the summer intern need to exercise sound judgment during the course of the summer in determining whether the relationship is going to work. It is better to

make that evaluation before certain career-changing decisions are made.

Recruiting and retention are ongoing, dynamic institutional processes that demand intentionality, openness and care. By approaching them as shared responsibilities, with clear strategies and honest communication, we can build a workplace where people can thrive, contribute and succeed in the long run, no matter the outcome.

Words of Wisdom for New and Experienced Lawyers

These days, law schools seem to be making more of a concerted effort to better prepare students for the realities of practicing law. This is true not only with respect to better developing their writing, research, drafting and oral advocacy skills, but also teaching them about the business of law. All of these tools, as well as good common sense, pragmatism and strong people skills, are vital to ensure that young lawyers hit the ground running when they begin their practice. Law schools seem to recognize this fact and try to help their students accordingly. At the end of the day, these capabilities enable students to be more competitive in the marketplace, which ultimately inures to the benefit of both students as well as their schools.

From David's perspective:

"Much has changed since I went to law school. For example, the rise of the Internet, smartphones, social media, and now AI, none of which existed when I went to law school. There has been a generational shift, with the Millennial generation currently the largest generation in the workplace, followed by Generation X, with Generation Z fast approaching. Gen Z now has more people in the workforce than Baby Boomers and is expected to become larger in number than Millennials. However, as much as things have changed, there are certain fundamentals that remain pretty much the same. The core classes taught in law schools, especially first year, remain the same, though law schools are increasingly offering more clinical and practical skills training courses. What does remain essentially the same

today is the pressure to succeed, to choose a practice area and to pass the bar exam."

One of the most important skills for a new lawyer to have is a fire in the belly. Christina explains, *"When I was the hiring partner for my firm, I met and interviewed many hundreds of law students who already had a track record of academic excellence and success. The common denominator among them was intelligence. However, I found that a strong passion for the law and intellectual curiosity, coupled with that fire in the belly, were not nearly as easy to find."* Those qualities translate to someone who combines both sheer intellect and a very strong sense of motivation to yield a high-performing individual whose attitude and desire to learn and succeed transform into top-notch work product and the delivery of exceptional client service.

David explains, *"As a mentor, and as a client, the number one attribute I would like new lawyers to possess is emotional intelligence. This includes traits such as self-awareness and social awareness, traits which enhance one's ability to provide strong, effective client service and to develop business."*

Other important skills for new lawyers to possess are the ability to write and research. While these are often considered to be two separate skills, they really go hand-in-hand.

The Importance of Business Classes

No matter where law students end up starting their careers after they graduate, it is very important for them to understand the business behind the practice of law. Virtually all lawyers will embark on a career path that touches business in some way, even though they might not expect it, so it is important to have a basic understanding of business principles. If you want to manage a firm or your own practice someday, or go in-house, you need to understand at least the basics of business.

It is also vital to understand your client's business since it provides the context within which their legal issues arise, and need to be addressed and resolved. We believe that every law school should require their students to take basic business classes such as business organizations, bankruptcy, creditor's rights and secured transactions. In addition, if you are not an accounting or business major, an accounting for non-majors course can be very useful.

Factors to Consider When Choosing a Practice Area

There are a number of factors you should take into consideration when picking a practice area. First, you need to follow your passion and focus on those areas that interest you. It is important for you to be intellectually curious about the practice you choose. You also need to gain clarity as to where you can realistically find the practice you seek. Some practice areas are only available at law firms, while others require you to work for corporations or the government. With each of those choices may come certain geographic and salary restrictions, so you need to know what you are willing to sacrifice to get the experience you want. We also recommend that you research the relative supply and demand for the areas that interest you to ensure that your employment goals are realistic.

Be honest with yourself about what you want to do, and the type of environment you want to do it in. Consider your long-term goals - being a large firm partner, going in-house, opening your own firm, doing policy work or something else. It is also important to understand that your interests and passions will change over the years, so you cannot necessarily know today what those will be 10 or 20 years from now.

If you decide that you want to focus on a couple of areas, you first need to have clarity as to what those areas are and to what extent there are synergies between them, and whether it is common for attorneys to focus on both at the same time. If so, it will likely be an easier endeavor. You must also figure out which employers will allow you to have such a dual specialization. If you are already employed, you need to consider how often your current employer has granted this type of request in the past, how successful others have been in following this path and whether there are any potential issues with doing so now. If you find that the areas in which you are interested do not naturally lend themselves to a dual specialization, you will then have to do a cost-benefit analysis to determine what you are willing to give up in order to have the career you seek. In some instances, you may have to change jobs to have the flexibility you want.

If your job requires you to focus solely on one area, pro bono work may give you an opportunity in a different area, to expand your skills. Practicing in-house, especially in a small law department, typically requires you to focus on multiple areas.

People ultimately end up in the practice area that is best for them. However, the right practice area for you is often not the one you initially choose. It is generally an evolutionary process, since your preferences and interests can change over time, as well as the types of opportunities that cross your path.

From Christina's perspective:

"I started practicing as an environmental/real estate lawyer but graduated into a recession. These areas were very slow when I first started working, whereas the intellectual property field was a burgeoning practice with demand far exceeding supply. As a result, I had the opportunity to split my time between the two groups for about a year, and then decided to switch into IP full-time as a second-year associate. This has been my practice area ever since. I know I made the right decision and waited until the right time to do it. Had I tried to switch earlier, I would not have been ready. There was a process I needed to go through to be mentally ready for the change, but once I made up my mind, the transition was an easy one and I have been happily practicing in this area for over 30 years."

From David's perspective:

"I chose to do personal injury litigation long before I entered law school. Several years into my career, I realized I no longer enjoyed doing that. After much soul searching and following a close friend's recommendation, I chose to go in-house. I did not truly understand what it entailed at the time. I learned on the job and quickly realized I enjoyed being an in-house generalist. After several years of experience as a solo in-house lawyer at two different companies, I developed not only the skillset of an in-house generalist, but the passion to be one. When the opportunity came to move to my current company, I knew it was exactly what I wanted and I pursued it. Almost 20 years later, I know I made the right choice. I handle a myriad of substantive legal areas, some I have a great deal of experience handling, some I get to do for the first time, and that is why I love what I do. I have learned that no matter what choices you make, your career will take you in unanticipated directions."

Nuggets of Wisdom for New and Experienced Lawyers

No matter where you are along your legal journey, here are some mentoring nuggets to support you in finding success and satisfaction throughout your career:

- **Work between college and law school.** David explains, *"I was focused on being a lawyer, and law school was the last remaining roadblock, a necessary hurdle to get past in order to start practicing law. At that time, school was just a game to me. I believe if I had taken a year or two off, I would have been able to be more focused on learning and gotten more out of law school. Maybe I would have learned at an earlier age to listen to my gut about what is best for me."*

- **Have a fire in the belly.** It shows you are intellectually curious, strive for the right answer and success in all that you do. It shows you are willing to go through a brick wall for your clients. It creates forward momentum in your professional career, keeps you engaged and on a steep upward developmental trajectory.

- **Make yourself indispensable.** This may be challenging, particularly as you are getting your career off the ground. All it takes is baby steps. Be the first volunteer when your team needs help. Consistently deliver great work product in a timely manner, and look for ways to bring something important and unique to the table. Dependability is the first step towards indispensability.

- **Ethics, professionalism and civility.** Ethics is a foundational cornerstone of practicing law. There are the established legal ethics we are bound by oath to follow. There is also right and wrong. Professionalism and civility are also cornerstones of our profession. Lawyers who treat others with professionalism and civility achieve better results for their clients, are more successful long-term, and enjoy practicing law more than those who are not. In many ways, it comes down to the old adage that *"you attract more flies with honey than vinegar."*

- **Soak it all up.** You are a blank canvas and have a wonderful opportunity to learn so much in a short period of time. Embrace the opportunities to learn and grow from as many people as possible.

- **Have integrity.** Be the person you say you are. Do what you promise to do. When you make a mistake - which you will because you are human - own it and fix it. Do not try to hide as that is when you get in trouble.

- **Listen more than you talk, it is a critical part of learning.** One of the most common mistakes we see is young lawyers who do not listen closely enough to what they are being asked to do. Be thoughtful in your interactions with clients and your supervising attorneys.

- **Have emotional intelligence.** It is one of the most important skills for success in today's professional world. Some people possess it innately, while others need to learn it through practice. Everyone can improve their EI. Ultimately, EI helps you navigate not only the world of office politics, but how to be persuasive, and how to reach the best resolution for whatever matter you are working on.

- **Have a client service orientation.** Understand what the client needs, the business context for the ask, what is at stake for the client, their preferred deliverable, and the required timing. The right approach shifts from one client or project to the next, so keep in mind that no one size fits all.

- **Everyone can benefit from one or two trusted mentors.** As a new lawyer, you need a safe person to ask basic questions that you may not want to ask a more senior member of your team because, quite frankly, it is scary and embarrassing. A good mentor is like a good coach - they are supportive, but they tell you what you need to hear, not necessarily what you want to hear.

- **Office politics can be a mystery as you start your career.** David explains, *"A little bit of brown-nosing never hurt anyone; too much will kill you."* Your integrity and ethics will help you know where the line is.

- **Develop your network early.** Push yourself out of your introverted comfort zone and robustly develop your network. As they say, your network is your net worth, particularly when you are in private practice.

- **When an opportunity presents itself, seize it.** If you can see the upside, overcome your fears, and visualize success, jump on it. In other words, step outside your comfort zone. The rewards in terms of personal and professional growth will be well worth it.

- **Success is driven by many factors.** Raw intellect is critically important. But you also need to have focus and passion for what you do to help differentiate you from others and to make yourself unique.

- **Always be yourself, and be self-aware.** Check in with yourself early and often, know yourself and your strengths and weaknesses. Give some thought to how others perceive you and what their motivations are. You may not always get it right, but it is better to think about it and to try to do better than to not try at all.

- **Be mindful and strategic in everything you do.** Some people just go with the flow, drift and let life carry them wherever the current happens to be heading at the moment. It is important to steer the ship to the destination that speaks to you and directionally where you want to go. Consider how you have been approaching your life and career. By taking control, you have a better chance of achieving the happiness and fulfillment you seek.

- **Life is short.** While often said, it is very true. It is important to love and believe in what you do, and to strike that delicate balance between the professional and personal that truly works for you. Every day is a new day and another opportunity to open yourself to new experiences, wherever they may take you. They may lead you to places you never dreamed of.

- **Find a way to strike a measured balance.** With focus, determination and a structure to your day, you can achieve balance. You just need to be willing to create and find joy during the day, both with the big as well as the little moments. They will recharge and rejuvenate you.

- **Keep a positive attitude and have faith.** Everyone's career has its ups and downs. It is important to keep perspective, particularly through the tough times, and to avoid making precipitous changes without thinking them through carefully. Making a change without thinking it through can often make a tough situation even worse.

- **Pay it forward.** We must all give thoughtful consideration to the legacy we will leave the profession. Being a mentor and confidante to others, doing pro bono, teaching and participating in thought leadership activities are just a few of the many ways to do this.

Comparing and Contrasting: In-House vs. Private Practice

While there are many similarities between in-house counsel and private practice attorneys, there are also important differences. In this chapter, we are digging into issues from both sides of the conversation, courtesy of our own experience and expertise, Christina as a partner in BigLaw, with a focus on intellectual property, and David as an in-house generalist.

As this chapter includes both sides of a conversation, we have chosen to present it in a question-and-answer format, to highlight these distinct points of view, and to help those readers who are weighing their options, desires and career goals.

Christina:

"It is a real testament to loving what I do that I have been practicing in BigLaw for over 30 years. I have chosen to continue working as a partner within private practice because it is interesting, and because I feel like my development and growth as an attorney and as a person have mirrored the way in which the firms I have worked at have grown and developed, including through geographic expansion to create global firms."

David:

"Being an in-house generalist is a specialty in its own right. It is not merely that every day is different. On any given day I might handle five or six different substantive areas - contracts, employment, real estate,

litigation management and a number of other areas. I get to be a counselor, a business strategist and a business advisor, but always from the legal perspective. I also get to work with really good, really smart people who are subject matter experts in their areas. They support me in what I do and I support them in what they do to accomplish our company's business objectives. And from a pure lawyer standpoint, I actually have the best client I could ever ask for - a client that respects and listens to its lawyers, and whose goal is to always do the right thing the right way. "

What lessons have you learned about yourself and each other as lawyers?

Christina:

"I have learned that there are a myriad of ways to define yourself as a lawyer and to carve out a career path that is most meaningful to you. When I look at the choices that David and I have made with our respective careers, they could not have been more different. David is now the happiest he has ever been in his career and I believe he is very well-suited to having a generalist practice. It really fits his personality and his professional interests and goals. I have learned a lot about him personally by watching him develop as an attorney and observing the professional setting in which he flourishes the most - which is to closely partner with his business colleagues and to deal with a wide variety of legal issues.

For me, I have learned that I am an experiencer, meaning that I enjoy having a wide variety of roles. My number one priority is delivering top-notch legal services to my clients and being their trusted advisor. That is the most important thing I can do for them and my firm. I have spent my career honing my legal skills so as to be effective in that role. There are a variety of other responsibilities I have had over the years at my firm that have enabled me to develop a unique skillset beyond just being a lawyer. I have had numerous meaningful leadership roles in various contexts, including within my practice group, hiring, pro bono, diversity and professional development. These roles have helped me to grow and develop as a professional and as an individual. They have also taught me that I can accomplish whatever I set out to do and that I can create a career that is unique to me and about which I'm passionate and committed."

David:

"I have learned a few things about myself. One is that I love being an in-house generalist, which is a far cry from what I thought I wanted to be when I was growing up. I have learned that life takes you places you never would have imagined before you get there and that your dreams, desires and goals change as you go through life - and that it is much easier and more enjoyable to embrace that change than to fight it. I have learned that I enjoy handling new matters that I have never handled before or, as I often describe it, I enjoy working outside of my comfort zone. I have also learned that I have good instincts, that I can and should trust them and that I do best when I rely on them.

About Tina, I have known her since she was a second-year associate and I have had the pleasure of watching her grow and mature as an attorney and become a leader both in her practice and at her firms. I have been a client of hers, so I know just how good a lawyer she is. Through it all, and especially through working together, her passion, her drive, her commitment to excellence and unwavering integrity never cease to amaze and inspire me. No matter what obstacles may be thrown her way, she overcomes them, moves past them and becomes that much stronger as a result."

How have private practice and in-house changed over the course of your careers?

Christina:

"Much has changed in BigLaw since I first started practicing in the mid 1990s. Technology has transformed the legal industry, starting with e-mail and the Internet in the mid to late nineties. Today, there is artificial intelligence (AI), social media and everything in between. This evolution has changed how we do our work, who does it and the legal and business landscapes in which we practice. Additionally, the current state of BigLaw is a byproduct of globalization and consolidation in the market. The substantive and geographic expanse of BigLaw firms did not exist when I first started practicing law. As in many industries, BigLaw continues to evolve at an accelerated pace, which enables the industry to keep up with the evolution of the business world and helps ensure firms remain competitive."

David:

"Both private practice and in-house have changed tremendously since I started practicing in 1987. How each exists today would have been unrecognizable back then. Throughout my career, the in-house world has been on an upward climb in terms of size, prestige and sophistication. In contrast to 1987, many lawyers today think about eventually moving in-house, and general counsel roles are considered prestigious destination career goals. Over this time, the quantity and sophistication of work handled by in-house departments has increased tremendously, and general counsel are an integral part of the company's executive leadership.

Simultaneously, the depth of partnership between in-house lawyers and their outside counsel has also grown. While much of the day-to-day legal work of a company is now often handled in-house, outside counsel provides important and specialized assistance. They help increase the depth of expertise in specialty areas such as litigation, mergers and acquisitions and other specialized work like Tina's role in safeguarding and leveraging intellectual property on a global basis."

What are the biggest challenges you face in your position?

Christina:

"Being a partner in a large global firm is rewarding, but is also very demanding. At the end of the day, we are in a service business, and our success is determined by the quality of the services we provide. There is a substantive aspect to it, as well as the timely delivery of the services. Because I have decided to go down this path with my career, and realizing the level of commitment that it takes to keep clients happy, I have a 24/7 mentality. It is truly like being a doctor of law. Some people are doctors and they get the call from a patient, I am a doctor of law and I get calls from my clients at all hours.

My philosophy is that I am very appreciative that clients have chosen to work with me. My mentality is to see clients as people and to have empathy for them; and to not only understand them as professionals, and understand the organization they work for in the context of the business, but also understand who they are as people. What motivates them? What inspires them? What are their trigger points? And, what keeps them up at night?

I think the biggest challenge is striking that balance in the way in which you spend your time, because time is a precious commodity. You must figure out how to do it in a way that you get the most out of life that you can, in a way that is most meaningful to you. For me, it is balancing my commitment to my clients, to my firm and to my career with my commitments to my family and my friends, as well as my personal desires. I am also very committed to bringing others along, whether it is folks in my firm, or in giving back to the community. For me, that is a critical part of who I am.

Being a woman in this profession is a blessing in many ways, but what I have found is there are often stereotypes. Being Latina in the profession and at the level I am at, at this stage, there just are not that many of us. When you look at not just women partners or diverse partners, but at diverse women partners, there are very few. Sometimes you have to deal with stereotypes. Part of it is navigating through a profession that is still mostly men, particularly the more senior you get, and having to deal with stereotypes and trying to break those down not only for myself but for other people, and that is part of the mentoring and giving back that I do.

Another challenge is keeping all of the balls in the air. There are so many responsibilities to juggle any given day, and my personal life often takes a back seat to everything else. But when I look at everything I like to do now and how much I get out of these experiences, I realize that a calmer existence would mean giving up things that mean a lot to me and which have been instrumental in my development. They are in addition to, rather than in lieu of, my day job. I am not willing to give those things up, at least not right now, particularly since these experiences help differentiate me in a profession that continues to reshape and redefine itself. It remains to be seen how the law will continue to evolve and who will come out on top and who will be left behind."

David:

"One of the biggest challenges I face is figuring out a way to say "yes" to my business clients. For example, when the client asks me to review a supply contract that is so incredibly one-sided in the customer's favor and exposes us to unreasonable economic risk, and my sales person says we cannot make any changes to it because the customer will not allow it and everyone just signs it as it is anyway – getting to yes can be a bumpy road but it is a ride I enjoy. You would be amazed how often that happens.

One of my approaches to practicing law generally and in serving my clients is that I make a real effort to demystify lawyers and the practice of law. I am part of the team and I am someone you can rely on to get the job done and protect our interests, as well as to keep the business moving. Another difficulty can be having enough time to do everything and turn it around in a reasonable amount of time - that is a constant balance. Another challenge is doing something new every day. I am often presented with substantive issues that I have never dealt with before. That is why I love doing this. For example, keeping up with the fast-paced changes and the scope expansion of different types of compliance and trade matters. These present the challenge to continue learning and improving my skillset, which leads back to why I said I enjoy practicing in-house. Over the course of my career I have developed good judgment and good legal instincts, and I have learned to trust my instincts and rely on them. That helps me get through the hardest part of pretty much any situation.

For me, one of the most difficult things that I have to do is field calls about employee issues that ultimately end up with the employee being terminated. Deciding when somebody has to be terminated is not a decision to be made lightly. You are making a decision that may ultimately end up with somebody not having a roof over their heads or food to feed their family. I try to save people's jobs when possible, but it is not always possible. I have been in-house for almost 30 years, and over that time the economy has gone up and down. In down economies, companies sometimes must lay off employees and reduce in force. Those are emotionally tough situations, but as lawyers, we learn how to navigate through them."

What do you wish the other side understood about your job?

Christina:

"I think the people who know me know this, but for those who do not know me, I wish they would know how seriously I take my job. My job is not just a job. For me, it is my life, and I see my job as being an attorney, a counselor, advisor, confidante and sometimes coach. The confidante part is sometimes like a therapist. With some clients, I develop a very strong

friendship. They will confide things in me from a personal standpoint because they know they can trust me, and I have their best interests at heart.

As part of being a partner in a law firm, because I am an owner of the business, I have a fiduciary duty to the partnership and what that means to me is that I have a legal and moral duty to put the interests of the firm first. To me, it is a tremendous responsibility and privilege and what it means is delivering the best client service I possibly can, because that will ultimately be in the best interest of the firm. I have a very strong loyalty to my clients and for being there for them through thick and thin.

The relationships are priority number one because at the end of the day, that is what we are all about. If you do not have a good relationship with your clients, then you may lose them at the drop of a hat. What is unfortunate is some attorneys give those of us in private practice a bad rap, which leads people to believe that all attorneys are out to make a quick buck. And sometimes people take that mentality to the next level and say when you are an attorney in a large law firm charging a certain hourly rate, that means you are out to make a quicker buck than if you are at a smaller firm. And that is just not true. Value is key, and while there is a quantitative analysis to it there is also a qualitative element to it. Separate and apart from sitting at my desk in my office or at home, speaking to clients on the phone and delivering services that way, or giving legal advice through some written means, I am constantly - 24/7 - looking for ways to make my clients' jobs and lives better and to make their businesses more lucrative.

To me, this is about making a meaningful difference. My brain never turns off. It is going all the time; even when I am not at work I am constantly thinking about it. I am dreaming about work. Some of the best thinking I do for clients is late at night or early in the morning when I am getting ready for the day. In the middle of a dream, I will think of an answer to a problem. That is a tremendous value to the client. I wish the other side would understand that this is beyond a job; this is a way of life."

David:

"I am a provider of substantive legal services. I am not a legal traffic cop. When I hire outside counsel, it is for the substantive expertise and to be my partner in helping me help my company, which is helping our client ultimately achieve the goal in the best, most expedient way possible. I am not hiring outside counsel to beat them up and knock down their bills.

When in-house lawyers are faced with legal issues, we are not looking at them in a legal silo. We are actually looking at a business issue that has a legal component. It is a constant balancing between what is the best practical legal answer versus what is the best practical business answer. In my world, the business answer is almost always paramount. I am constantly thinking about how the advice I give is going to direct the decision my businesspeople make, and how I am going to directly impact the bottom line of the business. My job is to mitigate the legal risk exposure, while keeping the business flowing. One of my favorite parts of practicing law is getting to know my client's business. And a lot of times people will say in-house attorneys are much better situated to learn about the client's business, and it is true to a certain extent. But it does not mean outside counsel cannot also learn the client's business and the culture. I think it is important for outside counsel to learn our business as much as they can."

How important is time efficiency between inside and outside counsel?

Christina:

"Now more than ever, there is an expectation that outside counsel will get the job done as quickly and cost effectively as possible. There is also a demand that matters be handled in an efficient, streamlined fashion, both from the account management and communications protocol perspectives. There is a general expectation to accomplish more in less time and with fewer resources. Maximizing your team efficiency is a critical part of that equation."

David:

"It is very important. This is driven by four primary factors: billing rates; reduced budgets; limited time and resources; and the 24/7 nature of the job fostered by modern technology. Efficiency is one of the essential elements of determining value, translating into the perception that the lawyer and the law firm take my concerns and interests seriously and are advancing my matter on its merits."

Is there anything about the other side's position that you are envious of?

Christina:

"The one thing I am envious of with respect to in-house lawyers is that they interface so closely with their business colleagues on a regular basis. This results in a level of understanding of their client's business that you ordinarily do not achieve in private practice - the business' needs, desires, pressure points, strengths, weaknesses and its long-term strategies and goals. This enables in-house lawyers to partner with their clients in a deeper, more meaningful way. Oftentimes, in-house lawyers are also able to wear other hats within their organizations, which enables them to get exposure to different aspects of the business that are not only interesting but which also provide tremendous learning opportunities outside of what one generally finds in private practice. I believe it would be a lot of fun to have those types of experiences."

David:

"I love what I do, and I do not want to go back to private practice. However, sometimes when talking with outside counsel, I get a bit envious of their depth of knowledge and expertise in their field. That being said, I

enjoy my specialty of being an in-house generalist and do not want to trade it for anything else."

What are your top pet peeves about the other side?

Christina:

"I feel very fortunate that I have a really good relationship with the clients with whom I work, and a lot of times it is not just a working relationship but a personal relationship too. Very rarely do things come up where we have to have a difficult discussion. But when we do, we are able to smooth things out.

There are a couple things that I have noticed from my perspective. First, there are sometimes issues with respect to in-house counsel believing that outside counsel do not really understand or necessarily care about the pressures they have to deal with in terms of being a company employee. Instead of being a revenue generator, they are a cost center within their organization and that sets up a dynamic that is quite different from a lawyer in a law firm who generates revenue for their organization. I know that there is a sense that by being a lawyer at a law firm, my job is easier because my job seems to be focused on getting to the right legal answer. By virtue of being in private practice for over 30 years, coupled with having the great experience of being seconded to two clients for a total of a year, I really do have a deep understanding and strong appreciation of the business issues that come into play when you are making decisions as in-house counsel.

For me, it is really important for in-house counsel to explain what the bigger picture is. If I am able to see the bigger picture from all the relevant angles it makes my job easier. My job becomes harder when I am given a small component of what the relevant information is - then I am not able to take into account the bigger picture and give the best advice. I think I am at my best with my clients when I am not only giving legal advice but when I am also able to transcend legal advice and give them advice on what tack to take with internal clients in terms of pushing the issue forward.

My third pet peeve is when the assumption is sometimes made that large law firm lawyers are always going to be more expensive than lawyers at smaller firms. That misconception is the result of the conflation of two concepts, which is the concept of hourly rates versus the ultimate value delivered to the client. There are a variety of ways in which large law firm lawyers can be less expensive and deliver better value than their small firm counterparts. For example, large law firms often have resources available that clients can take advantage of that may not be available at a smaller firm. The attorney who you are working with at the large firm may also be more efficient, so they are taking less time for whatever task they are doing. Large law firm attorneys will also sometimes work under some type of alternative fee arrangement, which may not be dependent on what their hourly rate is. There may also be myriad other perks that the large law firm lawyer can provide, which can drive and deliver value."

David:

"Poor work product. For example, if I hire outside counsel to draft a particular product sales agreement, please do not give me back a form contract that I could write in my sleep. If I hire you, it is because I need your expertise, which is something I do not have. If there is information you are not clear about, call and ask me. Make sure we are on the same page rather than guess and hand me poor work product.

Another pet peeve is slow turnaround, especially if I stated the urgency of the work. That includes responding to emails, and voicemails, as well as providing written work product in a timely manner. Because we are all busy, communication is key. I need it back with sufficient time to review. Emailing me a brief on the filing date is not sufficient time.

The last is billing issues. I billed time for a number of years and I understand that billing is difficult and time-consuming. For nearly 30 years, I have watched my wife spending many hours working on her bills. I know how much time she spends to get it right. However, some things do arise on bills from time to time. Things that bother me are entries that do not adequately describe the work performed; entries that do not belong to the matter on which they are billed; not including time spent on each activity described; charging me to leave a voicemail or a two sentence email; entries by lawyers and paralegals that I have never heard of and did not know were working the matter; receiving a bill for a 10th of an hour and it is the only thing on the bill; and billing for that initial consultation when I am trying to figure out whether to even retain you. What I always say to attorneys is, when you are issuing a bill, your ultimate goal is to make me happy to pay you."

What advice do you have for attorneys starting out in private practice or in-house?

Christina:

"There are a number of tips I recommend to attorneys starting their careers in private practice. Remember that you only get out of an experience what you are willing to put into it. Law is best learned through mentoring and guidance from others who are experienced. You should make an effort to get training and develop knowledge alongside your peers and create conditions that maximize the effectiveness of mentoring. Also, learn as much as you can as quickly as possible. It is important to develop relationships with both clients and colleagues, and keep an eye towards carving out a niche that sets you apart from others on your team. Also, do not wait until you are a senior associate or a junior partner to work on business development. Make an effort to develop relationships that attract business as early in your career as possible. It is the foundation upon which a partner practice is built and critically important for a long-term career in private practice."

David:

"To attorneys planning to transition from private practice to in-house, my first piece of advice is to check your ego at the door. When you were employed by a law firm, you were a revenue generator, and that is the most important person in the room. When you are working in-house, you are a cost center and a service provider to the business and sales teams. Developing relationships is as important for success in-house as it is in private practice. Make time to get to know your business and your colleagues; learn what your company does and how it does it; learn what your business colleagues do and how they do it. Build relationships and become a confidante and trusted advisor to business leaders. This will ensure your success within the organization as well as enhance enjoyment of your practice."

What qualities do you look for when you seek to hire outside counsel?

David:

"Before looking at specific outside counsel, I first have to consider the context of the matter. I consider various factors, including the nature of the matter, the economic value, the importance to my company and whether location is important. Once the context is clear, I will start considering outside counsel, and there are myriad qualities I seek. Most important is subject matter expertise. Other important factors are quality work product, client service, reliability, prior working relationship and reputation. I also look for lawyers who are passionate, creative and proactive. It is quite evident to me when I meet a lawyer who loves what they do. Working with a lawyer with these qualities not only makes it more enjoyable for me, I am more comfortable having the knowledge that my company will be getting the best representation possible."

How involved do you want in-house counsel to be after you have been hired for a job?

Christina:

"First and foremost, I want my client to be happy and satisfied with my team's work product and the client service experience. As part of that, I recognize that there is a certain level of engagement on the part of my client that will make them feel most comfortable, especially at the beginning of the relationship. I also know that our dynamic will evolve over time as we get to know each other and our respective working styles better. The business context will also dictate a certain level of involvement by in-house counsel, as well as the type of matter at issue and what is at stake for my client, both individually as well as in their own internal business relationships. My philosophy is to let the client drive this process and to keep open communication to ensure that there is an alignment of objectives and expectations on both sides."

How do billing rates factor into retaining outside counsel, and how do you judge whether the rates will translate into value?

David:

"Generally, rates are not the first thing I look at. I am more interested in hiring the best lawyer and firm for the project. I will assess the criteria I previously mentioned in the context of the anticipated value to be provided by the lawyer and law firm as compared to others under consideration. The billing rate is only one factor in determining the value proposition of any outside counsel retention. The higher hourly rate lawyer may very well be a better value than the lower hourly rate lawyer. Value, and the decision whether to hire a particular lawyer or firm, are decisions that cannot be made solely on the basis of an hourly billing rate. Furthermore, most lawyers and firms today are willing to consider a range

of billing options that will enhance the value proposition of a potential retention. Exercising good judgment to determine value is part of what I am paid to do as the in-house lawyer."

How do you balance the pressure to raise billing rates against the client's desire to keep those rates low?

Christina:

"It has always been a delicate balance. It is critical to stay focused on what really concerns and interests clients, which is the value proposition of the legal services you are offering. When engaging outside counsel, companies are looking for firms who demonstrate that they understand how that specific client defines value. Rates are just part of that equation. There are other metrics which are also very important to the discussion, including the level of experience of the service team, as well as how effectively resources are leveraged within that team and whether fee structures align with the client's expectations. These are just a few examples of ways to drive value that cannot be measured by hourly rates alone. Ultimately, the goal is to develop a model that is tailored to the specific context of the client and situation and which addresses the needs and goals of everyone involved."

What are the biggest challenges facing law departments today?

David:

"Though the details may differ depending on the size of the department and whether it is new or established, there are several overarching challenges, including risk management, data privacy/security, cyber crime, and regulatory compliance and incorporating AI into the practice of law and the organization as a whole are among the major challenges today. Resource issues, including staffing, IT resources, and outside counsel spending are also a priority. Defining value and ensuring

alignment between outside counsel and law department needs, including the critical connection between client service and budget/legal spending are key. For global companies and those going through acquisitions and dispositions, integration issues and differences in the legal frameworks across countries can be quite challenging. Focusing internally, ensuring alignment between the legal department and the businesses it serves."

What are some outside counsel's top priorities in ensuring a satisfactory attorney-client relationship?

Christina:

"There are a number of key priorities, such as understanding the client's overall business objectives and where its legal needs fit within that context. You need to figure out how the various tasks and responsibilities will be divided between in-house and outside counsel, and who will drive a given matter. Sometimes, outside counsel plays more of a supportive role to in-house counsel. And, at other times, those roles are reversed. As demands change, outside counsel must confirm that it can provide the client with all of the necessary resources. They must also be able to educate the client on what it will take to get the job done and ensure that there is consensus among all of the interested parties. There needs to be alignment on the likely outside counsel spend and how in-house counsel values those contributions. These discussions should happen as early as possible. The common theme across each of these points is effective, timely communication. Outside counsel needs to ask the right questions and listen carefully to the answers."

How are in-house counsel's needs likely to evolve over time and how can outside counsel effectively address them?

David:

"The details will vary depending on the law department. But I think one major theme applies across the board - increasing collaborative partnering between law departments and law firms. First, consider the evolution of in-house counsel over the past 30 years, from what many considered low-skilled, traffic cops to prestigious, destination positions attracting the best and the brightest. Today's in-house lawyers are talented practitioners. They know their client's businesses and handle a large amount of their client's day-to-day legal needs. Increasingly, they turn to outside counsel only when they need a depth of expertise, possibly a larger talent bench, to partner with on complex matters that are beyond the expertise or staffing capabilities of the in-house department.

Outside counsel should learn the client's business so they speak the same language and bring their expertise to bear in a more collaborative way. In-house departments are typically proactive; outside counsel needs to be as proactive as their client, thereby enhancing their collaborative partnership. To accomplish this, outside counsel should regularly visit their client's facilities; consider seconding lawyers in law departments; and conduct periodic reviews and feedback meetings to find out what works and what does not. Law firms should strive to be seen as an extension of the law department."

What are some of the most meaningful differentiators among outside counsel?

Christina:

"There are numerous differentiators, with the more obvious ones being the substantive expertise, quality and reputation of the outside lawyer

and law firm. Outside counsel's experience in the client's business sector is very important as well, since it provides the context within which the legal advice is given. Meeting or exceeding client expectations with regard to the value proposition is also very important, as well as being willing to share some of the uncertainty and risk with the client.

Clients do not want lawyers who merely punch the clock. They also do not want lawyers who are just talented technicians. They want trusted advisors who demonstrate a willingness to go the extra mile and are willing to put themselves in their client's shoes. This enables outside counsel to make their client's problems their own and to take ownership in resolving them. Outside counsel should also take the time to better understand the client's business and help foster relationships which could prove fruitful to them. These are just a few of the many steps which lawyers can take to develop an understanding and perspective that clients truly value and to garner a level of trust and loyalty that will set them apart from the competition."

Client Service: The Key to Success

Client service is receiving more attention and is incredibly important, particularly as the delivery of legal services continues to evolve. As a result, attorneys in private practice are competing much more aggressively for clients, and there is increased awareness that one of the most important things that distinguishes attorneys from one another is the level and quality of attention they give to their clients. Client service is the meaningful differentiator between good lawyers and great lawyers. It is the biggest thing clients remember about their experiences with a particular lawyer.

Client service is so much more than having a deep knowledge of the substantive area in which you practice and being able to get to the right legal answer. It focuses on taking that legal advice, viewing it holistically and putting it into a context that enables the client to make a sound business decision for their organization. While providing quality work remains of upmost importance, client service places a particular emphasis on developing more of a partnership and a collaborative relationship with your client. Just as it is important for outside counsel to provide outstanding client service to their clients, it is equally important for in-house attorneys to do the same with their business colleagues.

Emotional intelligence skills are a critical part of successful client service, including empathy, effective communication and listening skills, optimism and a proficiency at inspiring confidence and trust. The moment a client seeks advice regarding a new matter and the staffing process begins, it is prudent to include team members who have experience with, and institutional knowledge of, the client, since they can offer invaluable insight and guidance. They can also help frame the relevant issues in a way that draws upon past experiences with the client, their working style, their likes and dislikes, their strengths and challenges and their victories and defeats. Indeed, this is a unique value add that other team members may simply not be in a position to provide and which makes a world of difference when measuring the team's overall performance and effectiveness. To the extent that the matter is a new client engagement, it is important to determine who on the team has relevant substantive and business sector experience.

From the moment that a new engagement begins, attorneys should be evaluating not only what the client relevant legal issues are, but also the frame of reference of their primary client contact, both with respect to the matter at hand as well as within the context of the corporation or business unit in which they work. It is also important to determine who else within the client's business may be affected by the issue and whether it is necessary to involve them in any decision-making process. Budget and timing considerations should also be openly discussed and a preliminary plan developed so that there is consensus from the beginning and a framework within which to have continuing conversations regarding these parameters, particularly in the event the approach needs to be tweaked.

As the matter intake process progresses, lawyers need to determine not only how they are going to substantively address the legal issues at hand, but also how to package the results in a way that is most meaningful and helpful to the client. This requires a delicate balance between technical skills and emotional intelligence. Attorneys should confirm that they have the required expertise and knowledge to properly address both the legal and business perspectives, and determine whether they need to line up additional resources on the client service team, particularly as a matter evolves. Lawyers must be self-aware enough to recognize when bringing others into a matter may better serve the client than trying to do the work oneself, even if the project is within one's general practice area. Ultimately, doing what is best for the client, both in terms of quality and value, preserves and strengthens a client relationship, and includes not doing work yourself that is better done by someone else. Do not let your fear or insecurity about introducing other people to your client drive you to make decisions that are not in the client's best interest.

Once the client team is formed, the team leader must properly communicate the project scope, clearly define each member's role, conduct the necessary risk assessments, and effectively manage the project from all relevant angles. At this juncture, it is critically important to assess the exact nature of the necessary deliverables, beyond just the legal advice itself. Indeed, sometimes a client is seeking moral support or personal advice in tandem with the legal advice, and the high EQ lawyer will sense this and effectively serve as the trusted advisor that the client needs.

As the project winds down and the team prepares to advise the client, it is always prudent to take a step back and assess the team's performance and to consider the best way to deliver the advice. Every client and situation is unique, thereby requiring a carefully tailored approach. Ultimately, one must consider the impact the advice will have on various constituents within the organization, whether additional decision-makers and stakeholders need to be informed and whether the conclusion will require further research and evaluation. Even if the project has reached its natural end, high EQ dictates that attorneys follow up and seek feedback to ensure the client is satisfied.

The business world continues to rapidly evolve and this is the environment in which clients are forced to operate. The end result is a buyer's market for legal services where clients are requesting more for less and greater value than ever before. They are demanding more business-focused creativity from their lawyers. They are also demanding approaches to problem-solving which are more as a strategic business partner and advisor than an arms-length service provider. Clients also want their attorneys to significantly invest in their relationship. This means a strong commitment to developing the qualities and characteristics that drive all healthy relationships, including trust, loyalty and communication.

These client needs have brought about a more sophisticated relationship between in-house and outside counsel. David explains, *"I think the majority of in-house lawyers are interested in truly collaborative partnerships with their outside counsel. Successful outside counsel understand that, ultimately, we should be aligned with the same goals."*

Building Strong Client Relationships

Clients want sophisticated legal advice that is customized to their specific business needs and takes into account their risk tolerance. They also want their lawyers to deliver great value to their businesses, and they expect strong service. Lawyers need to understand that these concepts - great legal advice, value and exceptional service - mean different things to different people, so the trick is to figure out how each client defines them and how to strike the right balance so that the relationship is a success. The right blend of these characteristics constantly shifts within a given relationship. It is important for lawyers to be sensitized to these dynamics and to adjust their approach accordingly.

Whether the lawyer is retained for a single, discrete matter or an ongoing engagement, clients want targeted advice, delivered quickly, conscientiously, for as low cost as possible. Clients want their lawyers to help them solve their problems and help them manage risk to maximize business potential. They want their lawyers to be available when needed and to make them feel like they are their most important client. They want trusted advisors and to know their lawyers always have their backs.

There are a number of things which can jeopardize a relationship. Ultimately, they are all symptoms of a lawyer not meeting their client's needs and expectations. Over-promising and under-delivering is one of the most common mistakes. Giving legal advice in a vacuum and failing to adapt to the changing legal and business landscapes are additional missteps. Poor communication can also be a key mistake because of the potential consequences, including an inability to really hear and understand what a client is saying. These are the cornerstones of creating and maintaining a successful client relationship.

Another huge mistake is lying to a client. Don't do it. Poor billing hygiene, such as billing too much for tasks, or for things you should never bill for in the first place, is another quick way to lose your client's trust. For example, if a company's general counsel asks outside counsel to prepare a proposal for handling certain matters going forward, do not bill for that time spent. Another huge mistake is neglecting your client. Do not let your client think you have forgotten about them or their matter by going radio silent for long stretches of time. Check in once in a while, even if just to say, *"Nothing is happening, but here is what and when to expect something."*

Changing Conversations

The dialogue between in-house and outside lawyers has shifted considerably over the years, much in the same way that the practice of law has evolved. Bottom line: there are a lot more expectations in communication around the relationship, and what outside counsel is expected to deliver to in-house attorneys. There is a lot less tolerance for ambiguity, particularly around cost. For example, if there is a cost overrun for a particular project, outside counsel are expected to shoulder that risk much more frequently now than they used to.

Clients also really want to know up front who is going to be working on the project, beyond the relationship partner. They want to know how much time is going to be spent by the different levels of attorneys and other professionals, both as a cost check and to develop a rapport with the whole team.

The client's expectations around the final work product are also key. Sometimes the client is expecting a luxury car, sometimes they are expecting a scooter, and sometimes they are expecting a skateboard. It depends on the circumstances the client is in, what they need and can afford.

There are several important factors in getting to the root of your client's needs. First, you need to understand the issues your client is facing and the legal and business implications of those issues. To get to the heart of those issues, you must have open and honest communication with your client. You have to be able to ask the necessary questions and be willing and able to listen to the client's answers and hear what they are saying.

The correct legal answer only gets you halfway, since there is always a business context within which issues are addressed and decisions are made. There are also other factors, such as the client's organizational politics, which play an important role. Lawyers need to be sensitive to these dynamics and be able to strike the correct balance so that the advice they provide is from the most practical and constructive point of view for the client.

From Christina's perspective:

"One of my favorite aspects of this whole topic is the human interaction, right brain, intuitive angles to these conversations. The clients really need to feel like they are being heard. And they have to feel like their outside counsel is actively engaged in the conversation. If clients do not feel like their outside counsel really want to help them at the end of the day, and are just running the clock and wanting to get paid, I think that really shifts the conversation in a way that ends up hurting the client relationship. Sometimes what is not said is more important than what is said. Clients are charged with figuring out which of their outside counsel is driving value to the business and who is really driving great results. And there is an expectation among clients that their attorneys are going to be willing to take the time to understand their business. That they are going to be willing to make an investment, both in terms of time and emotion."

From David's perspective:

"The changes I have seen in the conversation really relate more to the structural elements of the relationship: more discussion about budgets, more discussion about alternative fees, more discussion about value, and evaluating the relationship. And I think these changes in the conversation are positive. They bring about value in the profession, generally, and in the attorney-client relationship in particular. If the conversations are had in the spirit of openness, honesty and trust, then it really is a win-win situation."

If you are having a fully transparent conversation and you are talking about different aspects of the relationship, you can gain greater budgetary certainty, better planning, and better overall communication, leading to a stronger overall relationship. These discussions can be difficult to initiate, especially if you have never had them before. But they are actually much easier to have than people might think. Resources such as the Association of Corporate Counsel (ACC) Value Challenge provide a terrific model in which to hold these dialogues. It outlines the beginning of the conversation, and it helps to frame the conversation in a mutually valuable way. It should be noted, these conversations are not just about cutting outside counsel fees. They are about shifting and restoring value to that relationship. It is about the processes and mechanisms that you can engage in to build value, which in turn lead to a stronger, healthier, longer-term relationship.

If you have not been actively having these discussions, or if you have not changed the conversations you have been having with your outside counsel or your in-house client, then we urge you to start. David explains, *"Two things I look for in hiring and staying with outside counsel are creativity and proactivity. If you initiate that conversation, you are demonstrating both of those things to me."* The worst thing that can happen is your client says, *"No thanks, I am really happy with the way things are."* But if you kick it off with simple questions like: *"Have you ever considered alternative fee arrangements?"* or *"How are we doing?"* that can lead to a more open and deeper discussion about things you have probably never discussed before, or at least not anything you have discussed in depth. And that can only bring about a positive change in the relationship.

Improving Your Communication Skills to Become a Better Lawyer

Communication skills are at the heart of every great lawyer, and they are a lawyer's currency. As with most things, the more you practice, the better you become at it. It takes a lot of hard work to be a good communicator, and it helps to have strong mentors to help you hone your skills. Much of oral and written legal communications is taking a lot of information and distilling it down into a clear and concise message that clients can understand, while steering them in a particular direction. Regardless of how you are communicating with your clients, it is important to carefully think about what you are going to say before you say it. You should consider not only whether the message is substantively correct but also whether you are saying it as effectively as possible.

You also need to think about your client's preferred style and method of communication. Everyone has different styles which need to be respected. When you are meeting with your client, outline what you are going to say in advance to help get you started. When you are writing to them, carefully think about and proofread what you have written.

One of the best ways to improve your communication skills is to listen - listen to other lawyers, and listen to your clients, not only to what they say but also to how they say it. There is a physical aspect to oral communication, which is as important as what you say, if not more so. Observe other's body language, how they deliver their words, in court, in client meetings and on the phone. Observe their facial expressions and gestures. Listen to their tone of voice and modulation.

The more you speak, the better of a communicator you will become, so practice that as well - speak at conferences, client meetings and board meetings. The bottom line is practice. And remember - you can always improve, no matter how long you have been practicing.

As with any relationship, there are both good communication practices between clients and outside counsel, and poor. It is an attorney's responsibility to gauge the proper cadence and scope of the communications that their clients expect. Every client is different, as is every matter. Outside counsel should ask the right questions and also have an intuitive sense as to what is appropriate in a given situation. This will help eliminate issues around poor communication such as communicating too much or not enough; making significant decisions without discussing them with the client first; and failing to properly prioritize developments in the matter for the client's consideration. There is often an optimal rhythm of communication, and it is outside counsel's responsibility to figure that out.

Another bad habit is not being communicative with your client at all and allowing the monthly invoice to double as a status report. There is little worse than a client receiving a bill for work they had no idea was being done, especially when it involves important developments and decisions.

There is a delicate balance between tracking the status of a project and micromanaging the work, particularly since one client's idea of micromanaging is another's belief that you are doing a great job. Our advice is to stay close to your clients and get a good sense of what they want and need.

Micromanagement happens when you do not fully trust or have confidence in the people with whom you are working. We recommend that you work with professionals whom you respect and trust so that this does not happen.

From David's perspective:

"I tend to be actively involved in all matters assigned to outside counsel but try not to micromanage. The level of my involvement in a particular engagement often is a matter of importance and trust. If I feel like I have to micromanage my outside counsel, push them to move them along or ask for an update, it likely means there is a trust issue and trouble brewing. If the lines of communication are open and flowing, this is not an issue."

Dealing With Opposing Counsel

It is essential that you are calm, cool, collected and respectful in your communications with an adversary, no matter how contentious the situation may be. You should try to avoid taking an inflammatory tone in your communications, since it is generally unnecessary and can often make the situation more difficult. People will mistake the need to deliver a strong message with yelling or screaming to get it across. Strong messages are generally best delivered in a calm, direct manner. As in your dealings with clients, it is also important to try to see the other side's point of view as best as you can. By putting yourself in their shoes, you will have a greater understanding of where they are coming from. By doing your best to fully appreciate both sides of an issue, you will be better positioned to reach a satisfactory resolution to the matter at hand.

Implicit in effectively communicating to the other side is first understanding what your client's goals are. You will encounter a number of different styles in opposing counsel, some easier to deal with than others, and you have to learn to roll with whatever you get. We strongly believe in the old adage that you attract more flies with honey than with vinegar.

Defining Value in Legal Services

Since time immemorial, product and service providers have been evaluated based on various criteria, both quantitative and qualitative. While certain offerings such as the proverbial widget more readily lend themselves to quantitative evaluations, value-based discussions have increasingly focused on professional services such as accounting, consulting and the law. We can all learn from those industries which have historically made purchasing decisions based on optimization analyses and processes.

From Christina's perspective:

"As both an industrial engineer and a lawyer, I have a deep understanding of the desire to standardize procurement evaluations for legal services through a more disciplined, consistent framework. But just as there are advantages to applying these methodologies in this context, there are also inherent limitations, particularly when they are used in lieu of a more qualitative analysis of the more nuanced facets of a particular legal provider's offerings."

At the cornerstone of these evaluations lies the concept of value. Value is defined as the relationship between the perceived benefits of an offering as compared to its cost. This relationship can be expressed as a benefits-to-costs ratio. If that ratio has a value greater than one, the benefits outweigh the costs, and if it is less than one, the costs outweigh the benefits. While this analysis seems easy, it is not as simple as it looks. Indeed, the concept of price is often mistakenly conflated with the idea of value, although they are by no means the same. While price is one factor, there are many other important considerations which are given insufficient weight, or completely overlooked in the process. A few of these are included here:

1. **Relevant experience and efficiency.** These are critical to the legal services value analysis. The more experienced we are, the better we understand the critical facets of a particular issue, and the more we can contribute. We will also bring a more heightened level of efficiency to the engagement than a less experienced lawyer, which is also very important when determining our value proposition.

2. **Understanding the client's business.** There are a variety of ways to achieve this, including having a consistent, experienced team servicing the client across all of its legal needs. If the engagement is new, we should invest the time to get to know the client's business and understand its unique likes, dislikes and pressure points. Having relevant sector experience can be very helpful in winning the business and getting a jump start.

3. **Client service excellence.** This is a must if we are trying to differentiate ourselves from the competition. Important considerations include ensuring there is consistent alignment with our client's work product expectations, as well as being as accessible to our clients as they need us to be.

4. **Sound judgment.** As lawyers, we are regularly asked to express our legal views regarding various issues. Being able to consistently express sound judgment, particularly in moments of crisis and

outside of our specific area of expertise, will make the difference between being a good lawyer and a great one.

5. **Keeping the lines of communication open.** This is essential in ensuring a client's needs are well met. We should carefully gauge the nature and cadence of our client's communication styles and adjust our approach accordingly. Our clients should also provide us with the necessary information and cues to enable us to effectively make these assessments and to adjust our approach as needed.

6. **Correct our approach in real time**. Great lawyers are able to regularly evaluate their performance and determine what they are doing well and what they need to work on. If we find that a certain approach is not particularly effective, we should not wait until our client says something - we should correct it in real time, before the client even sees it.

7. **Seeing around the corner.** Mastering the art of prognostication is priceless. Clients highly value our ability to keep tabs on all the moving pieces of a particular situation and to play out likely outcomes a few steps ahead of the game and to advise them accordingly.

8. **Taking the long-term view of the relationship.** Every client relationship is unique. Sometimes they start off slowly or in a narrow niche, and at times there may be more in it for the client than for us. If we are willing to take a long-term view of the relationship, we will increase our chances of being able to realize the longer-term upside and to better monetize the relationship.

9. **Success is a two-way street.** As in all good relationships, there is a give and take with clients. Generally, their needs come before our own. At the same time, we must run our business responsibly. While

there may not be alignment across all of our service offerings and a particular client's needs, effectively striking that balance will solidify our credibility and help ensure the longevity of the relationship.

10. **Inspiring trust.** While being trustworthy is a critical component of inspiring trust, we must also demonstrate our ability to seamlessly weave together capabilities, project an inner confidence, and have a commanding presence, particularly when meeting prospective clients. This will enable us to demonstrate our ability to serve as a trusted advisor, which is another significant differentiator.

Finding the Right Answer, and Answering the Tough Questions

The right answer is more than simply reciting applicable law, whether one is working with business clients on commercial deals or individuals on their personal matters. Ultimately, the right answer for clients is the answer that best serves the client's needs at the moment. Determining what the client needs depends on the facts and circumstances of the given matter, which includes a broad range of considerations.

The right answer depends on the client, the issue, how important the issue is to the client, and who will ultimately make the business decision. The right answer for one client may be completely wrong for another, and the right answer today may be the wrong answer tomorrow. It can also depend on where the client's organization is in its lifecycle. The right answer is generally the best answer one can get to under the circumstances, and is not just the correct legal answer. It also takes into account the political and business dynamics at play.

The process of working with clients to get to the right answer requires a few key considerations. You need to determine what the right answer is from a legal perspective, assuming there is one. You then need to consider the business and political dynamics that are at play for the client, and you need to know who the ultimate decision-makers and influencers are and how they will go about making the call. You also need to consider whether there is a track record for making these types of decisions and what the best- and worst-case scenarios are. The client's risk tolerance and the timeline within which a client needs to get to an answer are important too.

The best way to start is by trying to ascertain what the client truly needs. This begins with learning the relevant facts and a discussion about the client's goals. Then it is a matter of discerning how those goals mesh with the reality of the facts and law. Sometimes this means having a conversation with the client about possibly modifying their expectations, tempering them or perhaps expanding them, as well as discussing pertinent legal and business realities, often drawing upon your own career experiences. These conversations with clients - discussing and debating facts and law and ultimately reaching the right answer - can be some of the most rewarding aspects of your practice.

You need to know and understand your client. Putting yourself in their shoes can help tremendously - but you also need to take yourself out of the equation at a certain point and not make the right answer for the client be about what the right answer is for you. This is particularly true when it comes to issues such as risk tolerance, where the client may be willing to take bigger risks than we would or vice versa.

Timing is also key. The right answer for a client is generally the best answer you can get to with limited knowledge and often under extenuating circumstances. You often have to feel your way through it and rely on what past experience has taught you in similar situations. You should also remember the importance of asking the right questions. Do not be afraid to ask questions and to seek help and guidance, especially if the issue is outside your area of practice. Finally, remember that there generally is no one right answer, and what we are really talking about is the best answer under existing time constraints which more than anything is an optimization exercise across a number of different variables.

The number one lesson is to listen to your client. This involves more than listing a recitation of the facts. You must hear their concerns, goals, passion for the matter, urgency, commitment and understanding, or lack thereof, about the situation. Discuss and explain potential outcomes, positives and negatives and assess risk. Do not simply say *"no"* - offer alternatives. Temper your black letter legal advice with business and life realities.

Number two, put your ego aside. You may think you know the right answer but so may your client. In the business/commercial context, your client knows his or her business better than you do. However, your client may not readily know or appreciate the right answer in a legal context. As the attorney, we must guide our clients to the right answer by engaging in the right conversations. Remember to revisit these conversations because the right answer may change as a matter progresses, and do not be afraid to change course with your advice.

There are a couple of scenarios in which you may need to tell your client that you do not know the answer to their question. The first is when the client is asking a question outside of your substantive area. The second is when the issue is in your practice area, but the client is asking for a level of certainty that you may not be able to deliver off the cuff. When the client asks you, *"Can I do this?"* or *"Will I get sued if I do that?"* for an issue in your practice area, depending on the circumstances, those can be very tough questions to answer. Christina explains, *"More often than not, even if I do not have 100% certainty, I am able to get the client to a level of certainty that enables them to make the business decision they need to make given the legal risk presented."*

When you are talking about an issue outside of your specialty, you may or may not have a gut reaction about it. Generally, we will tell the client that we need to do some additional legwork to get them the answer they need. Clients are generally very appreciative of this candor, and would much rather you be honest in these situations.

David explains, *"If it is a more technically discrete area, I will tell my client I need to consult with outside counsel and get back to them, and there is no problem with that."* Lawyers cannot really give a 100% absolute answer all the time. Our job ultimately is to manage risk. Our clients are sophisticated businesspeople and they understand that risk is an inherent element of doing business. They are looking to us to give them the confidence to know that a risk is acceptable and appropriately managed. While we sometimes have to tell clients that we do not know what the right answer is, we have also developed trust and credibility, and they know that even if we need to do research or consultation, ultimately, we will give them sound advice.

Above all else, provide the type of client service you would want.

From Christina's perspective:

"When it comes to issues that I am not immediately familiar with, there are a couple of buckets that those fall into. The first are those issues that fall within my practice area that I might not have an immediate answer to. In those cases, what I will typically do is pull a treatise or do some quick online research, or I will talk to a colleague who is in my practice area who may have dealt with that specific issue. If we are talking about issues that are outside my practice area, given that I am at a global firm with many hundreds of attorneys who have different specialty areas, often the quickest and most cost-effective way for me to get answers to those questions is to pick up the phone and talk to somebody with that specialty. Even when I am dealing with issues where ultimately another partner in my firm will handle the matter, I still stay involved, especially if I am the relationship partner for that particular client."

From David's perspective:

"I have a strong foundation to draw upon when I confront new matters I have not handled before. I ask enough questions to make sure I understand the issue. Depending on what the matter is, I might do some online research, or put out some questions on one of my lawyer listservs and seek feedback from other in-house attorneys. I will also draw upon my experience. Even if I have not dealt with the exact matter before, I will likely have dealt with something similar. If it is a complex area requiring a depth

of knowledge I do not have, then I will go to outside counsel who has that expertise.

It is rare that any issue I deal with is purely legal, but usually a mix of legal and business. I will often talk to the businesspeople in my company and make sure I understand the business aspects of the matter. This is where being in-house gives me a distinct advantage because I have direct access to the business folks. Handling issues I've never dealt with before, for me, is where the fun is. The ability to conquer new matters I have never dealt with before is how I grow as an attorney to become a better counselor and advisor."

Clients need their lawyers to understand where they are coming from and what they are trying to accomplish. They should take full ownership of their work and view the relationship as a partnership. This attitude means that outside counsel view their client's problems as their own, so if there is an issue keeping the client awake at night, outside counsel should also be losing sleep. In-house counsel also expect their outside counsel to understand their business and to be able to put themselves in their client's shoes. They want creativity - to think outside the box and to come up with innovative, thoughtful solutions to get the business where it wants to go. Finally, in-house counsel want their attorneys to prioritize what is in the client's best interest.

From David's perspective:

"As an in-house attorney, I am both the client - with outside counsel, and the attorney serving clients - my business colleagues within my company. I work hard to deliver top-notch work product and also to provide a level of service that enables them to do their job more easily and effectively. I also practice with the goal of leaving my clients with a positive impression of lawyers and the profession. I work hard to make sure they understand I am part of their team and part of the solution to help keep our business flourishing. For example, I learn their operational needs and

explain how the legal aspects of the matter facilitate or hinder our business. If I have to say no to something, I do not stop there but also bring solutions that will help close the deal and ensure the business continues moving forward. I strive to make my client look good and succeed in their job and leave them feeling that I made a positive difference."

Helping Clients Assess Risk

There are several important steps in helping a client assess risk. First, since risk needs to be examined within the construct of a particular circumstance, you need to begin by properly defining the situation. You also need to understand the different facets of the issue, what the legal ramifications are and the business considerations at hand. This includes having a deep understanding of what the business ultimately wants to accomplish and how those plans and desires may be at odds with the path of acceptable risk for the company. You must also understand the level of risk the client is willing to take. Ultimately, you need to help the client to balance the trade-offs between accomplishing the business goals and mitigating risk. Christina explains, *"I think of reaching this balance as tuning a radio and dialing it up or down depending on what the client's risk tolerance is."*

Often, certain aspects of a client's circumstances will make it difficult to assess risk. This includes, for example, when the situation is evolving quickly, and it is hard to know exactly where things stand at any given moment. Furthermore, when a lot is at stake with a decision, it can often lead to key stakeholders waffling, which can make it more difficult to reach a decision. Having a lot on the line can also make it hard to determine who the ultimate decision-makers are. Also, if there are a number of significant unknowns in the situation, or if the client's risk tolerance keeps shifting, it can also be difficult to reach a decision.

It can also be a challenge getting the client to understand both the business and legal risks. Another challenge is in not having all of the facts, and simply not having control of all outcomes.

There are a number of things that you can do to help your clients properly analyze and make decisions in the face of risk. First, you and your client should be as fluid as possible with decision-making and understand that you are in a dynamic environment and circumstances may change a lot during the process. You need to make sure that you are working with the right person at your client's organization who has the ultimate authority to make the decision, or who at least has direct access to these people. Seek out the information and people you need to best help your client make a decision that is consistent with its risk tolerance, and be sure that you fully understand what that risk tolerance is. Understand the potential ripple effects of the risk presented and the ultimate decision reached, and the overall impact. Finally, you need to be prepared, expect the unexpected, and allow for some wiggle room.

Happy Clients

Driving client satisfaction is more of an art than a science. The idea is simple - we should all do what is necessary to keep our clients happy. We all know this can be much more difficult than it seems. What makes one client happy can drive another crazy, and while a particular working style may be ideal for some, it may be completely unacceptable to others. As with most things, there is no one-size-fits-all approach to keeping clients happy. It involves carefully weighing myriad factors and striking a delicate balance across various levers. By doing so, we can more effectively nurture and grow our client relationships, so that they endure over the long run.

The following are just a few of the many important considerations in keeping clients happy:

1. **Know your client and understand their business.** We hear this all the time. Nevertheless, when we read client satisfaction surveys and about general counsel pet peeves, these are major issues time and again. Empathy plays an important part in effectively leading client relationships and understanding how clients see our

performance. Clients are people too, and we need to put ourselves in their shoes when evaluating how we are doing. We must keep up with current events in their businesses and in their sectors to understand the business context in which their issues arise.

2. **Deliver great client service.** This is another client pet peeve. Great service goes hand in hand with understanding our clients and their businesses. It is incumbent upon us to gather the clues when discussing projects and discerning the business context in which they arise. The more effective we are at leveraging this information, the better we are at consistently delivering what our clients want and need.

3. **Know your client's pressure points.** We all have them - those things in life that drive us crazy. Whether it is litigation, an important transaction, or a run of the mill project, we must figure out what our client's pressure points are so we know how to effectively navigate the landmines of a particular situation and so that we can serve as better advocates and trusted advisors.

4. **Don't be tone deaf.** Effective communication skills are essential in every client relationship. This means knowing when to talk and - even more important - when to listen. It also means truly hearing what is being said, even when nothing is being said at all. Some clients are very outgoing and communicative, while others are more quiet and reserved. Whatever the case may be, we need to adapt to our client's communication styles and recognize that they can vary widely from one person to the next. This enables us to react appropriately in any given situation.

5. **Don't be a used car salesman.** All clients understand that outside counsel need to sell their services to be successful. Much of this effort is directed to existing clients. Indeed, studies in business

development strategies have shown that there is a much higher likelihood of driving additional work from existing clients than creating new relationships from scratch. Being effective in business development requires a certain amount of gravitas and finesse, as well as knowing when to put the pedal to the metal and when to ease up. Clients expect outside counsel to be realistic and to discern the right time and place to try to generate more business, and the right services to pitch. Under no circumstances should we be selling them the wrong make or model. It will annoy the client and diminish our credibility.

6. **Be confident, not arrogant.** Clients hire outside counsel to accomplish those things that they cannot do on their own. A critical component of a client's hiring decision is whether the attorney under consideration inspires and projects confidence. This is particularly important with high-stakes projects where we are being asked to do the impossible, or where millions of dollars are on the line. At times like these, being meek or insecure will not serve us well. But we also need to know when humility and a softer approach are in order. Being able to dial the confidence meter up or down depending on the circumstances is an integral part of successful relationship management.

7. **Be proactive.** Clients rely on us to clearly and carefully map the ways in which a particular issue may play out and to promptly prepare them for the good, the bad and the ugly. We must draw from our professional experiences and leverage them to be as proactive as possible. We should also tap our intuition for our clients' benefit. If we have misgivings about something, we have to figure out why that is and timely advise our clients.

8. **Know your strengths and weaknesses.** No matter how great we may be at certain things, we simply cannot be good at everything,

and we can always improve various aspects of our performance. Being aware of our strengths and weaknesses enables us to figure out our sweet spots, and where we may need someone else's assistance to navigate through certain situations and circumstances. Ultimately, we will improve our success with clients and our organization's top-line revenue by making sure we have the right horses in the race.

There are other resources that can help with your client relationships. If you know lawyers who have experience working with certain clients, they can provide you with valuable insight that you might not otherwise have. You can also reach out to experienced practitioners and mentors to get some general advice, and also do some research about your clients to better understand their businesses, successes and challenges. Finally, you should take a step back and think about how you would approach being the client and what you would want from your outside counsel. It is always helpful to put yourself in their shoes to predict their approach and needs.

What is unique for in-house counsel is that they are both clients as well as attorneys for the internal business teams. The challenge is to delicately walk the line as both lawyer and employee. You must remember that your legal duty runs to the company, not to any individual employee, which is not always easy.

Socializing for Success

Professional success hinges on a few factors, including the quality of the relationships that you have with your colleagues and clients. It is very difficult to build alliances and to develop the trust and credibility that comes with them unless you put yourself in situations where you are able to meaningfully interact with others and get to know them better. Work functions are often the easiest way to do just that. Having a level of comfort with your colleagues helps ensure that they will think of you the next time they have an issue that is within your area of expertise, and vice versa. It also facilitates other types of workplace collaboration, including leadership, business development, recruiting and integration activities.

These connections are critically important. People need to know you, like you and trust you or they will not want to work with you. Socializing and attending work functions together helps establish rapport and credibility with your clients and colleagues that are critically important to success on every level. When done with an open mind, such activities not only help build business, they can also enhance job satisfaction.

Partnering With the Business

Partnering with the business means working hand in hand with people at the client to effectively work through and manage both the legal and business aspects of a project. Whether our client contact is in the legal department or is a businessperson, it is all about understanding their priorities, objectives, strengths, weaknesses, pressure points and best- and worst-case scenarios. It is also understanding how each of these is defined for the client as an organization may be different from how our point of contact chooses to define them for themselves.

It can also be thought of as becoming an integral part of the business team, a valued partner in operations, development and strategy. David explains, *"I work as closely with our business teams as possible, from the senior most leadership on down, so that I learn as much as possible about every aspect of the business, including how our factories operate, what our customers' products are and our overall industry landscape."* The greater your understanding of these details and the big picture, the better lawyer you are for your company and clients, and a more valued and trusted partner for your colleagues.

Issues may arise if you are not picking up on the cues that your client is giving you, either directly or indirectly, about how they feel the situation would best be handled. Since the correct legal answer may not always align with how the client wants a situation to turn out, you need to be clear on the client's position so that you can adjust your approach accordingly. As part of that, you need to understand that if you find that the answer is "no" when the client has already decided to move forward, you should then quickly shift the conversation to one about risk mitigation, rather than just saying "no." You need to remember that as the lawyer advising the business, it is ultimately not your decision to make.

In sum, exceptional client service is not a luxury - it is every client's expectation, and its presence or absence is evident, no matter who the client is. The following tips will help maximize your effectiveness with clients, thereby deepening your existing relationships and facilitating your development of new ones.

- **Honor your word** - Clients will evaluate you and your services based on what you actually do on their behalf, not on what you intend to do or say you will do. Ultimately, clients will judge you based on how well your actions align with the expectations you have created in their minds, especially when their management is holding them accountable for your performance. There is nothing worse than overpromising and underdelivering.

- **Be responsive** - Clients both appreciate and expect their attorneys to be responsive, even during evenings, weekends, vacations, and while traveling. They also expect timely follow-ups once their immediate needs have been addressed. Business happens 24/7, 365 days a year, and attorneys need to be just as responsive as their clients are required to be. You can be a terrific lawyer, but if you are not there when your clients need you, you may as well be mediocre.

- **Listen to your clients** - Listening is a critical skill, particularly when getting assignments and receiving feedback from clients. You need to be able to hear and process what they are saying, recalibrate your approach to the extent necessary, and go back to your client promptly to communicate solutions. Even in challenging situations, you can strengthen your relationship if you are thoughtful and strategic in how you react and communicate.

- **Go the extra mile** - You must be generous with your time and genuine in your willingness to help your clients, even if you do not reap immediate rewards. Successful business is all about relationships which are cultivated and deepened over time and through connecting with others in a meaningful way.

- **Build a strong team** - You cannot do it all alone; you need to hire and mentor your team to understand, appreciate and develop strong client service. You are only as good as your team, and teams are more effective when everyone cooperates, participates, collaborates and brings others along.

- **Build on your strengths** - It is always important to be open to feedback, both positive and negative, and to learn and grow through professional and life experiences. It is just as important to celebrate your strengths, and to determine effective ways to leverage those talents as much as possible, rather than focusing on remedying your weaknesses. You cannot be everything to everybody and, at a certain point, trying to do so becomes counterproductive.

- **Be empathetic** - Effective client service requires you to always put yourself in your client's shoes and think about how you would feel if you were facing the issue at hand, both from substantive and contextual standpoints. Often, it is not just a legal problem that needs to be addressed; there is also a business context within which the issue arises which requires just as much attention and consideration.

- **Focus on the deliverable and the audience** - Package your work product with care, and remember that reaching the right answer is often only half the battle. Figuring out the framework within which to deliver the advice can make all the difference in whether the client will consider your performance a success. Is your client looking for a bottom line, no-frills answer, or do they need something more formal and elaborate? Who at the client organization is the ultimate audience for your advice? What kind of relationship do they have with your client contact, and where do those individuals fit within the context of both the issue at hand and the organization as a whole?

- **Stay positive and be authentic** - Clients can tell when you are being open, honest, authentic and trustworthy, and they are much more likely to respond in a loyal way. If you are pretending to be someone you are not and do not genuinely care and put your clients first, it is obvious, and clients respond accordingly. Being positive and upbeat is just as important, and showing that you love what you do will make you more attractive to both existing and potential clients.

- **It is about more than just being a good lawyer** - Client service excellence is about so much more than just great technical abilities; it is about exhibiting emotional intelligence, which is priceless to clients. There is no other way to cultivate successful client relationships than to inspire trust, and the most effective way to do so is to build a meaningful foundation by exhibiting a high EQ. As professional services expert David Maister so aptly stated, *"Ultimately, hiring a lawyer is about confidence and trust. It is an emotional act."*

Professional Development

Choosing your career path can be a challenge. It requires a great deal of thought, strategy, planning, perseverance, patience and risk tolerance. First, you need to gain clarity on the type of career or practice you want — simply knowing you want to pursue a particular career or make a change from your current career path is not enough and can actually lead to a premature decision and jeopardizing your existing job in the process. You need to do your homework.

You should map out why you are interested in a certain area and consider the potential risks, rewards and different courses of action available to you. Is your current employer a viable option in helping you to reach your goals? Also consider talking to others who may be helpful in navigating these waters.

If you are seeking new challenges at the office, you must first be open to them. If you welcome these possibilities, they will begin presenting themselves, and you will then need to be prepared for them. In order to create space for them, you should periodically examine all of your current responsibilities to assess whether they are the highest and best use of your time, or whether you should try other things. You may develop a more efficient way of doing things, or identify other people to whom you can transition some of your work. This will not only free you up for other activities, but will also give you the opportunity to mentor others and help them to develop and grow.

David explains, *"My job is similar to Chicago's weather - wait 5 minutes and it will change. New challenges find me, I also go looking for them. I read about changes in the law and trends in the profession. If I think we need to implement something new, I talk with my General Counsel about it."*

The Power of Networking

Many of us view networking as an effective vehicle for improving our careers. However, you first need to figure out your short and long-term goals and plans - how much time do you have for networking, and how can your current contacts or those whom you want to meet through your network help you accomplish your objectives? You should then strategize as to when and how you are going to connect with those individuals and periodically examine how successful your efforts are to figure out what works well and what can be improved. Remember that networking is a two-way street. Just as you are seeking help from others, you must also be willing to assist them along the way. Often the individuals you help today are the ones who will be there for you tomorrow.

Success, in both your career path and with clients, is about building relationships. Your network needs constant nurturing, not just when you are looking for clients or a new job. It takes time, often years, before you reap any benefits from certain relationships. A strong network enhances your professional and personal life, leads to new opportunities and enables you to make a difference for others.

Changing Course Within Your Current Organization

What does moving up mean at your organization? What positions are available if you did so, and is this something you want for your career? You need to assess the roles, responsibilities and requirements for promotion, and you need to consider whether your skillset is a good match or if you need to do some work in certain areas first. Consider consulting with your mentors and trusted advisors, both within and outside the organization, who can be a good resource in helping you determine whether your expectations are realistic and in helping you develop a strategy to accomplish your goals. Are you willing to put in the necessary hard work to be patient and flexible? Promotion opportunities sometimes take a long time to materialize.

In the meantime, are you the best you can be in your current position? Demonstrate that you are a leader and a team player. Take initiative and follow through. Gain the trust of others in your organization, so that they will support your advancement. As professionals within service-based industries, your primary goal is to serve your clients and your colleagues well.

Education and Self-Improvement

Another way to explore a career transition is to go back to school and study a particular discipline. An MBA, LLM or a certificate in a particular business field or substantive practice area are just a few examples and can help accelerate a career pivot. Furthering your education is never a waste of time and can only serve to improve your professional skills in whatever field you choose to pursue.

The Importance of Diversifying Your Skillset and Wearing Different Hats

Diversifying your skillset means expanding your capabilities beyond what you do on a daily basis. It can take a number of different forms, including developing substantive knowledge in additional areas beyond your main practice area so that you become adept across several different subjects. It can also mean acquiring and honing skills in other areas such as leadership, client service or business development which may not directly contribute to your bank of knowledge but which are nevertheless important in making you a better professional and person.

It is essential that you are thoughtful and strategic in how you go about diversifying your skillset. While there is little if any downside to proactively seeking out new and different opportunities, it is important to guard against being too scattershot in your approach. There are only so many hours in a day, and a self-improvement plan needs to be carefully balanced against the demands of your current job and other facets of your life. You need to take a step back and think about your high-level goals and objectives and why you are interested in developing certain skills, and what the best way to go about doing so is given the realities of your schedule and existing commitments. When you are open to new and different work experiences, you become well-positioned in diversifying your capabilities, which enables you to learn and grow.

There are many reasons to diversify your skillset. It can help you to more adeptly handle a wide array of tasks and to do a better job of issue-spotting. To the extent you are looking for a new job, it can help you to more effectively differentiate yourself and makes you more marketable. It can also contribute to your overall job satisfaction and help keep you from getting bored. It also better prepares you to interact with many different people and leadership styles.

Wearing different hats enables you to round out your skillset in a way that staying in the same role does not. It also helps you to figure out what you really like and want for your career. Sometimes you have no idea that you like something until you have the chance to try it. Moreover, what you want and need from your job evolves over time as you grow and mature. Wearing different hats allows you to explore different aspects of yourself while at the same time meeting new people and gaining a better understanding of various facets of your organization and the business world at large.

Living Outside Your Comfort Zone

You should never let yourself get too comfortable or complacent. Living outside your comfort zone means regularly engaging in activities which enable you to meaningfully stretch and grow. Another way of looking at it is being an "experiencer" — someone who likes to go out and try new things, even when they are scary. There is a certain amount of self-confidence and fearlessness that you gain as a result, both of which are an important part of being successful.

On any given day, you may deal with a broad range of issues across multiple substantive areas. While you cannot be an expert in each of these areas, you must be able to address them all in a way that drives the results you need for your business, with minimal risk exposure. Many professionals will tell you that their success is due in large part to developing a comfort zone with being outside their comfort zone. Christina explains, *"Some of the best opportunities of my career have come from making myself do things I never thought I could."*

Living outside of your comfort zone helps keep you from getting bored and enables you to diversify your skillset. You avoid being perceived as a "one-trick pony," which will open doors and tee up opportunities that may otherwise not be available to you. It also helps you build your stamina and gives you the ability to take on more duties and responsibilities. This is particularly critical when you are interested in pursuing leadership opportunities. David explains, *"When I first joined the Association of Corporate Counsel (ACC), I was so shy that I actively avoided the networking portion of programs to avoid talking to people I didn't know. Fast-forward 13 years, and I was president of the board of the ACC Chicago chapter, which is comprised of other very smart and talented attorneys who looked to me to lead this very successful 2,000-member chapter for a year. Getting out of my comfort zone and becoming involved in activities like these helps to develop many skills, especially the soft skills essential to leadership and career success."*

As professionals, your clients do not call you for the easy, routine issues they can handle on their own. Rather, they are going to call you with issues that, at least once in a while, will initially stump you. You need to embrace the challenge, go outside your comfort zone, get creative and solve their problem. Issues do not come neatly packaged in readily identifiable and solvable single-issue boxes. There are always new and unique twists that are just different enough, and what we have done before may not be the right recipe this time. You have to go somewhere new and different - outside your comfort zone.

It is always important to take calculated, rather than reckless, risks. This requires a lot of thought and planning. That being said, do not underestimate the value of going with your gut when it comes to making important decisions about ways to stretch yourself. Pushing to the next level is not easy and can be very tiring and stressful. It can also force you to face your inner demons, which may sometimes get very uncomfortable. But when you come out on the other side of the fear, you are much better for it. Stepping outside your comfort zone is scary at first, but ultimately exhilarating and rewarding.

Reinventing Yourself (A Professional Rebirth)

When done in a professional context, reinventing yourself means that you are adding to your skillset in a way that is meaningfully different than before. It is a profound shift in who you are and what you do. This could mean changing or expanding your specific industry focus, or your entire career. Reinventing yourself takes discipline, focus, patience and a lot of hard work.

To successfully reinvent yourself, you first need to have clarity about how you want to do it and your reasoning behind it. This will ensure your intentions are well-founded and that you are undergoing this transformation for a reason. Then, you need to figure out what steps you have to take to get there. You should break this process into smaller steps, then map out what you have already done and where you need the most work. For example, taking classes, reading books and speaking to others who are knowledgeable about a new area can help provide important guidance. Mentoring is also crucial and invaluable during these times of transition. Sometimes, just jumping in and taking on a new role is the best way to learn, like riding a bike. There is often no substitute for just stepping into a new set of responsibilities and owning them.

It is important to make conscious choices and to be an active participant rather than an observer in the process. You also need to make sure this transition makes sense for you and that it is something you truly feel passionately about. These changes usually take a lot of work and are done over a period of time, so you need to be both patient and realistic about what you want to achieve. Also, maintain your focus as you juggle the responsibilities of both your current position and those along the path toward something new. Keep your head in the game.

Transitioning your practice can be difficult substantively, financially and emotionally, so you must think critically and do your homework. Do not just leap to your friend's idea of a dream job, chase the hot area of the month or simply follow the money. You will not be happy and will soon be longing to reinvent yourself once again. Think carefully about why you want to transition — is it the particular job or the practice area?

Reinventing yourself also makes sense when you are no longer enjoying what you are doing and do not feel a strong sense of fulfillment. It is also a critical step along the path to meaningful growth and is particularly key in the leadership context. Many great leaders have gone through a number of significant transitions over the course of their careers in an effort to make themselves more well-rounded, nimble and ready to take on the most senior-level positions in their organizations.

From Christina's perspective:

"During college I worked at several retail record stores and as an industrial engineering intern in the microcircuits factory at Motorola. It was a terrific job as a student and offered a glimpse of what my life would have been like as a full-time engineer. I realized it would have been interesting and well within my sweet spot but not enough to enable me to stretch and grow the way I wanted — so I chose to attend law school instead. In law school, I worked as an intern in the legal department at Baxter Healthcare, and as a summer associate at a now long-defunct law firm. Since graduating from law school, I have worn a number of different hats including leading different client teams; working on-site at two clients for about a year; leading the Chicago office and national hiring teams for many years; having

leadership roles within my practice group; being on the steering committees for my firm's equity and inclusion and women's initiatives; being a member of executive and policy committees; being a legal and business columnist for a number of publications; and a podcaster. Each of these roles has played an invaluable part in who I am today as a professional and person, even those jobs that you would not think immediately translate into a career in the law. They all served in starting new chapters in my professional development and have provided me with the opportunity to meaningfully diversify my skillset."

From David's perspective:

"I began my working career at age 15 cleaning floors in a lamp shade factory and then worked at a restaurant during college. Since graduating from law school, I have been a new associate/first-year lawyer; I mention this because it is important to remember that is where we all started. I worked at four different law firms before going in-house, handling both defense and plaintiff's personal-injury and complex tort cases. I began my in-house career as the first in-house lawyer for a startup consulting company in the technology sector, creating both the legal and human resources departments from scratch. From there, I went to a small electronics manufacturer where I was again the sole in-house attorney. I am now an attorney for a family of companies in the steel and aluminum manufacturing sector, doing business all over the world. I have been a board member for different nonprofit organizations, including a homeless services agency, a charter high school and a bar association, including holding various officer positions, including president. These course changes have taught me many valuable skills and allowed me to make good friends. I have also been able to become a leader in the in-house bar and make a positive difference for my colleagues, something I did not initially set out to do but am greatly honored to have been able to accomplish."

Advice From the Authors

From Christina's perspective:

"Be creative about the options you are considering, but also be realistic, particularly about the amount of time that is required to take on a new role. You should also be strategic about the roles you explore — think about the skills that you have and those which you are trying to develop and how best to acquire them. It is also important to give full consideration to whether your employer can offer you the opportunities you seek and whether they would otherwise be supportive in your efforts to acquire these skills. Getting new/different experience does not necessarily mean that you need to find another job. Sometimes you can take on different roles with your current employer or by working with an outside organization.

There are a few lessons I have learned along the way that I wish I had been told earlier. First, while a career in the law can be very rewarding, it can also be all-consuming, and it is important to pursue outside hobbies and interests too so that you can be a happier, better-balanced person. You also need to consistently look for ways to stretch and grow as a professional. While many lawyers often equate this with learning different areas of the law and taking on a wide variety of work projects, it is also just as important, if not more so, to develop your soft skills. People who are truly good at both can be hard to find and are the ones who tend to find more professional and personal success and satisfaction in the long run.

I have been the beneficiary of a lot of great advice over the years. One thing that immediately comes to mind is when I was told to channel my interest and proficiency in math and science into studying engineering in college. Having this background has been a game-changer for me, even though I did not ultimately have a career as an engineer. It has enabled me to look at the world and its perplexities through a very different, more discerning lens, which gives me the opportunity to bring something unique to the table. I am also a firm believer in the importance of following your passion, which was some great advice I was given a number of years ago."

From David's perspective:

"Do not be afraid to try new things. If you don't try, you may well miss out on something you truly enjoy. My career is a good example. After doing personal-injury litigation for several years and essentially burning out on it without a backup plan, I jumped in head-first to become an in-house generalist without any prior experience, only to learn that I both love and excel at it. I think most lawyers find their specialties by serendipity rather than intention. Trying new roles is one of the best methods to accomplish this.

I received some outstanding advice along the way, particularly from my father. What I truly wish I had done is follow his advice sooner. My father's advice actually is the bulk of the advice I now pass along to others - to treat everyone well and as your equal, because they are and because you can learn from everyone, and to keep an open mind and learn as much as you can about as many different topics as possible, as everything affects the practice of law, in ways you cannot necessarily anticipate. It will help you be a better lawyer."

Mentoring and Executive Coaching

As the business world continues to be extraordinarily competitive, it is more important than ever for professionals to be at the top of their game. A professional's performance is now measured by much more than just how good they are technically. Indeed, clients evaluate and hire based on many other, more subjective characteristics. However, these skills are not always taught in school, and their importance is often undervalued during a professional's formative years. Yet these are the very attributes that differentiate merely solid performers from high performers - the good from the great.

One key ingredient to professional success is powerful mentoring relationships. These partnerships enable a mentor and a protégé to meaningfully collaborate toward achieving specific, well-defined career and personal goals. Mentoring can take a variety of forms, both formal and informal, and is free of gender, racial, ethnic and age restrictions.

Developing a Circle of Trusted Peers

There are organizations that are created for this very purpose — to provide membership opportunities to professionals who wish to formally become part of such a circle. But for those who wish to develop this type of circle more organically, it requires a combination of focus, strategy and serendipity. Focus comes from thinking carefully about what you are looking to accomplish professionally through a peer circle, and being determined and willing to put in the hard work to get there. You also need to be strategic in figuring out how best to get there and not leaving fulfillment of your goals to chance. Serendipity often factors in when, for example, you see that old acquaintance who happens to know someone you really want to meet, or by landing a speaking opportunity with a trade association that has many representatives from companies with whom you would like to do business. But remember — you have to be alert and open-minded to notice when serendipity is working its magic in your life.

From David's Perspective:

"The most significant trade group in my career has been the Association of Corporate Counsel (ACC). I joined when I first went in-house in 1999, primarily for the educational and substantive resources. I remain active because of the professional and personal relationships I have made. I am able to bounce not only substantive legal questions off of my contacts, but to also obtain career and situational advice. Volunteering with not-for-profits is another avenue that can help develop a circle of trusted peers and also provides an opportunity to learn from others outside your specific profession."

What is Peer Mentoring?

Peer mentoring means looking to contemporaries, both at work and elsewhere, to provide you with the support, guidance, perspective and assistance you need to develop professionally. Just as important, peer mentoring provides you with the opportunity to fill that role for others as well. As you get further in your career, it often becomes more difficult to find what we call the more traditional mentors - those who are "older and wiser" and with whom the traditional lines of teacher and student are clearly drawn.

Peer mentoring provides an opportunity for continued growth for each of us, albeit in a context that recognizes our depth and breadth of experience, while at the same time acknowledging the importance of learning. You can glean a tremendous amount by having conversations with different business leaders and others within your company, and you can learn at least as much simply by observing the way they conduct themselves in different situations and audiences.

While sharing substantive professional expertise is an important part of mentoring, the emotional intelligence of both the mentor and mentee is critical to the overall success of the mentoring dynamic. The most effective mentoring draws upon the mentor's ability to identify his or her own emotions and those of others, manage both sets of emotions, motivate oneself and others, and manage the overall mentoring relationship. The mentee must likewise exhibit these types of soft skills to maximize the relationship's effectiveness.

Advantages of Peer Mentoring

There is a lot of wisdom and guidance that we can all gather from those around us. Getting this type of coaching from others can be particularly helpful when they have encountered similar situations, successes and obstacles, and when those experiences are at least somewhat contemporaneous with ours. There are significant advantages to sharing these types of stories and anecdotes with peers both within and outside of our organization. There is also the intel gathering aspect to peer mentoring, which includes learning helpful information about other businesses. Finally, peer mentoring is a terrific exercise in building relationships and can often lead to meaningful networking.

In order to be the best we can be in all aspects of our lives, we must constantly strive to learn and to better our skills, both substantively and interpersonally. Gaining insights from your professional colleagues is one of the best ways to accomplish this, and to remain current with what is happening within your organization and your industry.

How To Be an Effective Mentor

Effective mentors have a number of key personal attributes. These include being authentic, candid, non-judgmental, empathetic, committed, inspirational, positive and successful. Mentoring is a form of supportive coaching; rather than focusing on a mentee's weaknesses, mentors should focus on enabling the mentee's strengths to foster growth and to see the magic in themselves.

At the outset, mentors should choose their mentees wisely and set the tone of the relationship to ensure that there is alignment of attitudes, goals and expectations. Both must speak the same language and, since the most effective coaching styles differ from person to person, mentors must discern which method will work best for the mentee. There should be agreement up front as to how the success or failure of the mentoring relationship will be measured. In addition, a dynamic and communicative environment must be created where feedback is both openly offered and willingly received. Confidentiality is a critical part of developing and maintaining mutual trust.

Mentors should provide concrete, practical tips on successfully navigating through various types of substantive and political issues within the mentee's organization. Mentors serve as sounding boards, and their candor is particularly important, especially with the more delicate issues facing the mentee. In addition to sharing specific tips and guidance, mentors should share war stories, which often provide the most memorable teaching. Indeed, sometimes the best lessons that mentors can impart are about their failures and what they learned as a result, rather than their successes.

As the relationship develops, mentors should remember that the ultimate goal is to enable the mentee to flourish and grow to their full potential, whatever that may be, even if the mentee ultimately takes a very different path than the mentor. Mentors must remain mindful that these relationships are not meant to last forever. In fact, some of the most effective mentoring occurs under a fixed timeline of limited duration, which helps ensure that the mentor and mentee stay focused on the specific goals of the partnership. Mentors should be sensitive to signals as to when the relationship has run its course and should carefully determine how best to wind it down in a timely, constructive and thoughtful way.

How To Be a Successful Mentee

A successful mentee is appreciative, courageous, eager to learn, flexible, open-minded, resilient and self-confident. They have a clear vision of what they hope to achieve and are likewise discerning in choosing their mentor. They realize that some of the best mentoring relationships are ones that develop organically and informally, and are open to such experiences. Mentees should be willing to step outside their comfort zone and are well-served to seek experiences from a wide variety of people, including ones with whom they have little in common but who nevertheless have much to teach. In fact, cultivating a number of mentoring relationships over time is an invaluable way to learn and share a variety of perspectives and styles.

Mentees should be active participants in the mentoring partnership; the dynamic should be one of both give and take. They should be willing to break old habits and develop new ones by taking the coaching and working diligently to ensure that they are actively integrating the mentor's advice into their lives. Mentors can provide mentees with a number of benefits, including access to their professional contacts, and mentees should understand the importance and value of developing this aspect of the relationship. They should also be mindful that mentoring relationships are just one component of an effective professional development strategy, and mentees should contemporaneously seek other types of opportunities by which they can learn and grow.

Finally, mentees should show appreciation for their mentor's generosity and should remember the importance of "paying it forward" by sharing their knowledge and experiences with other professionals.

While mentoring requires a significant commitment of time and resources by both mentor and mentee, it provides an effective, meaningful way to assist professionals in their career advancement. This investment is also a fundamental part of an organization's leadership development and succession planning; it is invaluable in positioning it for future success.

Exploring Executive Coaching

There are a variety of ways that professionals can effectively drive self-improvement and success. On-the-job training and mentoring are two primary development techniques. However, it becomes increasingly difficult to continue growing at a steep trajectory throughout one's career solely relying on these methods. One must often look to other, more creative ways to hone the necessary skills to become better professionals, role models and people. Executive coaching provides one such mechanism. It has long been used by organizations in developing their high-level executives and individuals being groomed for those positions. It is a form of professional development and mentoring which provides a framework and context within which professionals can assess where they are and where they are headed.

Executive coaching performs a number of valuable functions. It helps you to prioritize what is important to you, develop a strategy for reaching your goals, and implement an action plan using that strategy. Coaches take you from theory into the real world and help you identify your strengths, weaknesses, self-limiting behaviors and blind spots. They give you honest, real-time feedback and provide accountability, support and candor in a way that most other people cannot. Coaches see you in the same way others see you, and one of the core aspects of the relationship is teaching you that, for better or worse, other people's perceptions of you often drive your experience in the world.

Coaches ask powerful questions designed to elicit answers that will fundamentally impact the coaching process. The relationship must be built on trust and confidentiality - without them, it will fail. As Harvard Business School Professor Thomas Delong states, *"Coaches are truth speakers - they tell you what you need to hear, not necessarily what you want to hear."* This is critically important, particularly as you grow into a more seasoned professional, since it becomes increasingly difficult to obtain this information from those with whom you work, particularly when they are people who report to you. Coaches also function as good sounding boards and are committed to your success, no matter how you choose to define it.

It is important to understand what coaching is not. First, it is not a substitute for therapy or other forms of treatment. Sometimes there are issues that need to be addressed by certain types of trained professionals such as psychiatrists or doctors, not by coaches. Depending on your specific needs, coaching can actually do more harm than good if you are not receiving the appropriate help you need. In addition, coaching does not provide a quick fix to your issues and problems. Rather, it is a process of self-discovery and self-development and takes time to unfold.

If a coach is promising quick, easy answers with little or no effort on your part, you should carefully consider whether the coach is truly qualified. You must also be open to constructive criticism, to follow the process wherever it may lead you and to change your attitudes, habits and behaviors, particularly when they are self-defeating or destructive. You should bring your goals and desires to the process, rather than expecting your coach to tell you what they should be. Good coaches are not focused on their own agenda, or on that of the organization paying for their services. Instead, they only think about you and what you are trying to accomplish. In addition, coaching is not meant to dwell on the past. Although it can be helpful in figuring out what has and has not worked for you, coaching should be focused on creating a present and future that you want.

Picking the right coach is critical to a successful experience. There are many who claim a great track record and proven techniques. Unfortunately, it is often difficult to discern whether this is actually the case until you start working with one. Like all of us, they each have their strengths and weaknesses, some of which may or may not complement your own. For this reason, it is often better to start by speaking with individuals you know who have successfully worked with executive coaches, who can provide you with some insight into the process and who may be able to give you good referrals. It is important to then interview those coaches whom you are considering and to get a clear idea of their personalities, working style, what they envision for your coaching experience, and the types of professionals with whom they typically work. You need to both like and respect your coach. Otherwise, they are unlikely to get to know you in the way that is necessary for the process to truly work.

Finally, you need to figure out your budget and what type of coach you can afford. It is important to consider the frequency with which you intend to meet with your coach as well as the likely overall duration of the process. You should budget for some extra sessions in case unexpected issues come up requiring additional sessions. While working with a coach may stretch your budget, the benefits are often dramatic, long-lasting and well worth the investment. It is a truly transformative experience that invokes positive changes in the way you see your career and life, and the way that others see you.

Your Personal Brand

Personal branding boils down to how we show up in the world, both professionally and personally. It is not just about what and how we sell ourselves, but also about who we are. Many people define personal branding in two ways: as their reputation, and as the external markers that distinguish them. In our experience, it is both, and then some. Personal branding is about carving out a space in the world that reflects not just what we do, but who we are. It is about aligning our values, strengths and stories with how we show up in our careers, communities and relationships. When done authentically and intentionally, our personal brand becomes one of the most powerful tools to shape our lives.

Everyone has a personal brand, whether they are intentional about it or not. It already exists in how people experience, talk about and remember us. The question is not *if* we have a brand. It is *what* that brand says about us, and whether it is authentic and truthful.

Your Personal Brand Is More Than a Business Card

Personal branding is not just having a good headshot or a polished resume. It is how we carry ourselves, the energy we bring into a room, how we treat others and whether we follow through on our commitments. It is the substance of our character, the style of our dress, and the integrity behind our handshake. In short, our personal brand is the story people tell about us when we are not in the room.

Building an authentic personal brand starts with self-awareness and being brave enough to own it. It is about leveraging that self-awareness into clarity and consistent action. We become memorable, relatable and respected when we are grounded in what makes us different and allow those differences to shine through our words and actions. That is the kind of personal brand that endures.

First Impressions Matter—But So Does What Comes Next

First impressions are extremely important. People form impressions within the first few moments of meeting us and, for better or worse, those early judgments can be hard to change.

That is why it is so important to always start strong. Show up looking and acting the part, and you must also make sure the substance backs up the style. A sharp outfit might turn heads, but what we have to say, and our consistency, reliability and authenticity, are what build trust over time.

Simply looking successful is the easy part. Being successful is the long game. That means doing great work, treating people with kindness and respect, and aligning our actions and values, even when it is hard. Over time, synchronizing our values and behavior cements a personal brand people believe in.

Authenticity Takes Work—and Courage

Building an authentic and strategic personal brand requires effort, authenticity and discernment. We cannot just slap on a shiny persona and expect it to hold up. If we simply copy someone else's style, or pretend to be who we think others want us to be, we will end up disconnected from our own truth. Worse, people will feel that disconnect, eroding our credibility.

Instead, we need to spend time reflecting on what makes us who we are. What are our natural strengths? What are we passionate about? What unique perspective do we bring to the table? Answering those questions helps us to build a personal brand that feels honest, energized and deeply authentic.

All of this is not without risk. It means standing out, taking a stand and being seen, all of which can feel scary, especially in competitive industries where blending in might seem to be the safer approach. But when we take strategic, heart-centered risks, we are not simply building stronger brands; we are attracting the people and opportunities we want in our lives.

Evolve or Fade

Like many other areas of business development, personal branding is not a one-and-done effort. It is dynamic, and it must grow and evolve as we continue to stretch ourselves holistically. What worked five years ago might not reflect who we are today, and that is okay. It is necessary.

Personal branding must also be dynamic and fresh so that others do not get bored and think of you as a one-trick pony. As you evolve, both as a person and as a professional, your personal brand should likewise evolve. In the process, it is important to strike that delicate balance between being interesting and multifaceted and being seen as lacking focus. The key to successfully accomplishing this goal is intentionality, honesty and self-awareness. When we are clear about our work and values, people can follow our journey, even as we pivot, expand or reimagine what we offer.

The Internet Is Watching

The Internet and social media can be incredibly powerful tools for building and promoting our personal brand, but they come with responsibilities. While we cannot control what others post about us, we can control what we put out into the world. That is why we must be mindful, consistent and thoughtful about our online presence. Do periodic Internet searches of yourself. Review your social media and online posts and profiles. Be intentional about the platforms you use, who you connect with and what you share online. We live in an age of viral communication, and once something is posted online, it is out there forever, for better or worse.

Used wisely, social media can amplify our message, connect us with new audiences and position us as thought leaders in our field. But it only works if the online version of us authentically aligns with the real-world version.

Know Your Audience—and Speak to Them

A strong personal brand is clear about who it targets. We cannot be everything to everyone, and trying to do so will only dilute our message. Instead, we need to be discerning. Who are we here to serve? What do they care about? What do they need to know about us?

This is where the business development aspect of personal branding comes into play, not in a pushy, pitchy way, but in a grounded, relational way. When we know our audience, we can tailor our messaging and presence to resonate with them, while still staying rooted in our authentic selves.

We are not just building a personal brand that makes us feel good, but building a bridge between who we are and the people we are meant to serve.

Build It. Share It. Live It.

Once we have refined our personal brand and identified our audience, we must then put ourselves out there. That means seeking opportunities to speak, write, collaborate and contribute. It means saying yes to leadership roles and community engagement, and showing up - on purpose, and with purpose.

Our workplaces, networks and communities - both in person and virtual - are all places where our personal brand can shine. Educating others about who we are and what we offer gives them the tools to connect, refer and collaborate with us. Over time, that visibility inevitably creates opportunity.

Your Brand, Your Power

Personal branding is about empowerment, not ego. When done right, it is done with heart, strategy and integrity. An authentic personal brand is a way to align our inner truth with our outer presence and, in doing so, opens doors that lead to deeper connections, more fulfilling work and lasting impact.

Stop waiting to be discovered. Tell your stories, showcase your strengths and shape how the world experiences you. Your personal brand is already showing - and now is the time to make sure that it is telling the right story.

EMOTIONAL INTELLIGENCE: THE KEY TO STRONGER LEADERSHIP, RESILIENCE AND CONNECTION

Emotional intelligence (EQ) plays an essential role in the long-term professional success for individuals and the organizations they serve. While technical skill and subject-matter expertise are essential, they are no longer sufficient. Today's high-performing professionals must also master the soft skills that allow them to connect, collaborate, lead and adapt. At the heart of these soft skills lies a solid foundation in emotional intelligence.

What EQ *Really* Is (and Is Not)

EQ is not just about being pleasant, soft or agreeable. It is not about avoiding conflict, nor is it about suppressing your emotions to appear professional at all times.

Emotional intelligence is about *awareness*. It is about understanding your own emotions and regulating them, as well as "reading the room" - sensing the feelings of others, and then responding in a way that demonstrates and leverages that awareness to strengthen relationships, rather than fracturing them.

From Christina's perspective:

"When I started leading teams, I learned quickly that knowing the 'task' wasn't enough. I had to understand how each person approached a task, what motivated them, what made them feel seen, and what shut them down. EQ helped me shift from being a good communicator to a trusted leader."

Why Emotional Intelligence Matters

Popularized by Daniel Goleman in his groundbreaking 1995 book *Emotional Intelligence: Why It Can Matter More Than IQ*, emotional intelligence focuses on a framework of competencies that drive leadership performance and human connection. Goleman's model identifies four key components:

1. **Self-awareness** – Recognizing your own emotions and how they affect your thoughts and behavior.

2. **Self-management** – Controlling emotional responses and adapting to changing circumstances.

3. **Social awareness** – Sensing and understanding the emotions of others.

4. **Relationship management** – Influencing, inspiring and collaborating effectively while managing conflict.

These are not innate talents reserved for a select few. They are competencies that can be learned, practiced and refined over time, and are closely tied to other success-critical qualities like resilience and intuition.

We have all met people who are technically brilliant but emotionally tone-deaf. They might know what needs to be done, but their delivery lands like a lead balloon. Conversely, someone with strong EQ can often defuse tension, build rapport and inspire action, even when they do not have all the answers right away.

Emotional intelligence can be a game changer. It helps us navigate complexity, build trust and achieve better outcomes, not just faster ones. Every meeting, conversation and email thread has an invisible layer of emotion, nuance and energy. Emotional intelligence is the skillset that enables us to *read* that layer and *respond* appropriately.

From David's perspective:

"High EQ is what transforms a good professional into a great one. It separates someone who can just do the work from someone who understands the work's context, how it affects people, how it is received, and what success looks like for the client. EQ helps us feel our way through uncertainty when logic alone cannot give us the answer."

EQ in Action: Building Better Relationships at Work

Relationships are the foundation of every thriving business. Whether you are leading a team, serving a client or partnering across departments, EQ is the bridge that connects you. We rarely work in isolation. We are constantly engaging with executives, support staff, salespeople, vendors and clients, and they all have different communication styles, needs and pressure points.

EQ helps you to:

- Recognize and regulate your own emotional responses

- Understand other people's perspectives, even when they significantly differ from yours

- Adapt your style to fit the context, not just your comfort zone

- Navigate conflict with curiosity rather than defensiveness

David explains:

"Say a client walks into your office after you have had a rough morning and asks what sounds like a ridiculous question. EQ allows you to pause, recognize your own emotional state and still choose a constructive

response. That pause can help you save rather than destroy a relationship, and help you uncover what is really being asked beneath the surface."

Emotional Intelligence in Leadership

In challenging times, the ability to wear multiple hats and lead with empathy, adaptability and clarity is more valuable than ever. Leaders with high EQ often display:

- Strong communication and active listening skills

- Creativity and flexibility in problem-solving

- Optimism and confidence in the face of uncertainty

- Ability to inspire and develop others

- Conflict resolution and team-building expertise

Studies confirm that emotional intelligence directly impacts professional success. According to research by Travis Bradberry and Jean Greaves (*Emotional Intelligence 2.0*), EQ accounts for 58% of performance across all job types. Moreover, 90% of top performers score high in EQ, while only 20% of low performers do.

These statistics amplify the value of EQ-based training in areas such as mentoring, client service, leadership development and organizational culture.

Emotional Intelligence and the Power of Connection

EQ does not simply help us bounce back; it also empowers us to build trust, strengthen teams and inspire others. The ability to deeply understand and connect with people is a hallmark of high-EQ professionals.

Empathy, the ability to see the world from someone else's perspective, is one of the most undervalued leadership tools. Compassion goes a step further: it is empathy paired with the desire to take meaningful action. Together, these qualities create a sense of security and respect that cannot be manufactured.

Emotional intelligence begins with listening, not simply to what is said, but to what is not. It means tuning in to nonverbal cues, sensing emotional undercurrents, and making space for others to show up as they are. Emotional intelligence sharpens your ability to discern the full scope of any interaction. It helps you navigate conflict with curiosity instead of combativeness, and to collaborate more effectively by prioritizing connection over control.

No matter the setting - a team meeting, client pitch or performance review - the ability to manage one's own emotions while understanding the feelings and needs of others is often the difference between stagnation and evolution.

Technical expertise might get you in the door, but EQ keeps you in the room.

Managing Different Personalities with EQ

One of the most valuable aspects of EQ is the ability to read the room. Even if the "room" is just a single person, you can learn to understand someone's personality, emotional triggers and communication preferences. You can avoid miscommunication, respond instead of react, ask better questions, and defuse tense situations. This does not happen by accident. It takes observation, intention and effort, and with practice, gets easier over time.

Christina notes:

"I have learned to pay close attention to what people do not say. Their body language, the tone of their emails, and how they respond to

feedback give me clues about what they value and how they want to be engaged. EQ means constantly gathering data - not to manipulate, but to connect more meaningfully."

Difficult Conversations and High-Stakes Situations

The truth is that not every conversation is going to be easy. Sometimes we have to deliver hard feedback, and sometimes we are on the receiving end of someone else's frustration. EQ gives us the tools to stay grounded and *choose* our response rather than be driven by impulse.

When facing a tough interaction, consider these approaches:

- Acknowledge the emotion in the room without escalating it

- Ask questions that shift the focus from confrontation to collaboration

- Hold space for someone to be upset, without letting it derail your presence

Christina adds:

"When someone is being aggressive or abrasive, I have found it disarming to say, 'Are you okay? Did I catch you at a bad time?' Those questions often stop people in their tracks and remind them that there is a human on the other end of the conversation. It is not about confrontation, it is about connection."

Resilience Begins with Self-Awareness

Resilience, the ability to recover from setbacks and persevere through adversity, is one of the most essential skills in the modern professional world. According to the Mayo Clinic, resilience is the psychological and physical ability to cope with tough events and keep moving forward. People with high emotional intelligence are generally more resilient.

Why? EQ begins with self-awareness. It allows us to recognize our emotional reactions, assess whether they serve us, and then recalibrate our responses. This self-knowledge gives professionals the clarity and presence to stay grounded when everything else feels chaotic.

When a deal falls through, a colleague disappoints or your strategy implodes, emotional intelligence gives you the inner tools to pause, reflect and respond rather than react. It helps you step outside your frustration long enough to take the 50,000-foot view and ask the critical questions. What really matters here? What is still possible?

As Goleman teaches, understanding yourself is the foundation for managing yourself and connecting meaningfully with others, even under stress.

Resilience in Action: Tools for the Tough Moments

Resilience is not about ignoring your emotions - it is about working with them constructively and effectively. Some situations call for compartmentalization, a healthy coping mechanism that allows you to temporarily set aside frustration or hurt to address the task at hand. Other moments require a reset - a walk, a workout, a favorite TV show or even a few quiet minutes with a pet to recalibrate. These small acts of self-care make a big difference. They signal to your nervous system that it is okay to pause.

You do not have to power through every challenge like a machine. Resilience does not mean suppressing emotion. It means knowing when to feel it and when to shelve it. That discernment only comes with self-awareness.

The professionals who thrive are often those who can acknowledge stress without being derailed by it, and who can see a setback not as a failure but as feedback. One of the best ways to train this mindset is to follow

Stephen Covey's advice: *"Begin with the end in mind."* This means visualizing your desired outcome and reverse-engineering your path forward from that perspective. This forward-facing approach keeps you solution-focused instead of stuck in what went wrong.

The Role of Intuition

One of the most overlooked elements of emotional intelligence is intuition. It does not always get top billing in business circles, but intuition, or the ability to make decisions based on insight that is not always linear or data-driven, is a powerful asset. Merriam-Webster defines intuition as "quick and ready insight...without evident rational thought." Carl Jung framed it this way: *"Intuition does not denote something contrary to reason, but something outside of the province of reason."*

In practice, intuition often manifests as a gut feeling shaped not by magic but by experience, pattern recognition and emotional intelligence. High-EQ individuals are better at reading the room, sensing tension and picking up on the subtle cues others miss. That is not a coincidence - it is emotional data being processed at a high level.

In an era dominated by analytics, intuition still matters. Numbers can reveal trends, but do not always tell the whole story. Context, culture and nuance matter too. Great leaders do not rely solely on spreadsheets - they also trust their gut when appropriate. Intuition helps fill in the blanks when data is limited or incomplete. It brings humanity back into decision-making.

As Albert Einstein famously said: *"The intuitive mind is a sacred gifts, and the rational mind is a faithful servant. We have created a society that honors the servant and has forgotten the gift."*

The professionals who stand out learn to balance both.

Building EQ: A Lifelong Practice

Emotional intelligence is a practice, not a finish line. It requires ongoing reflection, self-regulation, empathy and curiosity. But the payoff is immense: stronger relationships, deeper fulfillment, and more sustainable success.

When you invest in your emotional intelligence, you are not just boosting your career; you are elevating your impact on clients, colleagues and your community. EQ helps you show up as a complete human leader who can think critically, feel deeply and lead with both heart and strategy.

In a world that often rewards speed and efficiency, emotional intelligence reminds us that connection, compassion and resilience are not luxuries, but leadership essentials.

We also live in a world where automation and AI can do much of the technical heavy lifting. What remains irreplaceably human is our ability to connect, understand, influence and lead with emotional intelligence.

Whether you are a seasoned executive, a new manager or an entrepreneur, investing in your EQ is one of the smartest moves you can make. It is not just good for your career; it is transformative for your relationships, leadership and sense of self.

The next time you are in a high-pressure moment, a challenging conversation or trying to decode someone's cryptic comments, pause, tune in, choose empathy and let EQ lead the way. Emotional intelligence is not just a tool for a better career - it is a blueprint for a better life.

Quiet Strength: The Power of Introverts

This chapter is written from Christina's perspective as an introvert.

A number of years ago, I attended an event featuring Susan Cain, author of *Quiet: The Power of Introverts in a World That Can't Stop Talking.* She spoke about her book, which is the distillation of many years of research and what she discovered about introverts, and herself, in the process. As a closet introvert, meeting Cain and reading her book were watershed moments for me. It was the first time I had encountered a mainstream discussion about something which had been personal and hidden for me, and the conversation was being framed in an open, frank and enlightening way. Her book gives introverts a meaningful voice, provides her audience with an insight into what makes introverts who they are and sensitizes readers about the importance and contributions of introverts, particularly as leaders.

Interestingly, Carl Jung and many other psychologists claim that all individuals display both introverted and extroverted tendencies and that no person can be just one to the exclusion of the other. Moreover, people's tendencies often change over time. Indeed, I have spoken to a number of rather extroverted individuals who have told me that they have become more introverted as they have gotten older.

There are many introverts among us. Cain writes that at least one third of the people we know are introverts. This statistic is significantly higher among lawyers. I have read that more than 50% of lawyers are characterized as introverts on personality tests such as Myers-Briggs. Given that so many of us are introverts, we need to be self-aware enough to acknowledge this about ourselves and to think about how this impacts our day-to-day lives and interactions with others.

I have spoken with several professionals who consider themselves introverts and have expressed interest in exploring ways to cope as one, in what by every measure is a very extroverted world. My takeaway from these conversations is that the discussion about introverts remains an important one that resonates with many. Indeed, there still remains much mystery and intrigue about what makes us introverts tick. We are among the most misunderstood in society, particularly when we spend most of our lives donning extroverted clothing.

One of the most important things we can all do is to understand and respect the different personality traits of those around us. While people do not always demonstrate the same set of traits across personality types, certain tendencies often manifest themselves. For all of you extroverts out there who are interested in better understanding the introverted contingent in your universe, here are some tips for working and living with introverts:

1. **Understand what being introverted means.** Being introverted simply means that we recharge our batteries by being alone rather than by being with others. This tendency often manifests itself through our work habits and how we choose to spend our free time. If we do not get enough alone time, we can feel run down and edgy.

2. **Understand what being introverted does not mean.** An important part of successfully interacting with an introvert is understanding what being introverted does not mean. For example, it does not mean that we are shy, nor does it mean that we are aloof. It also does not mean that we are arrogant, or that we do not like people. We are just like everyone else - we just need more alone time than many.

3. **Introverts are quiet - but that does not mean we do not have anything to say.** While we may not be quick to speak, it does not

mean we do not have an opinion. It simply means we are gathering data points and want to hear from others first before formulating our own opinions and taking the steps to express them.

4. **Introverts have good listening skills.** Introverts tend to do a lot more listening than talking. We also tend to be perceptive and notice details that many others may miss. This is just how we are wired. As a result, we may arrive at ideas and solutions that are a bit different than the average person but that nevertheless meaningfully contribute to the bottom line.

5. **Introverts are deep thinkers.** We are very analytical and try to see all sides to a particular situation before making a decision. During our quiet time, we are often thinking about a variety of issues on parallel tracks. This is what we tend to do in lieu of talking to others.

6. **Introverts can be hard to read.** This is because we are quiet and often do not speak our minds freely unless we are with others whom we know well and trust. Our silence can also be misconstrued for something more than what it is; after all, we live in an environment of perpetual stimuli. This is not only exhausting for the typical introvert, but others tend to think that something is wrong when the introverts among us are not enthusiastically contributing to the barrage of communications. If we can all keep in mind that introverts are just a bit more reserved, and nothing more, others will be less likely to misread where we are coming from.

7. **Crowds often make introverts uncomfortable.** Do not get me wrong - introverts enjoy being with people. We just tend to prefer one-on-one communications or being in small groups, particularly with people whom we already know. Introverts do not usually enjoy engaging in idle chit-chat, and instead seek a more meaningful connection with others.

8. **Introverts need time alone.** It is an energy thing. When introverts have spent a lot of time with other people, particularly those whom we do not know, it can be a physically draining experience. We need time by ourselves to recalibrate and re-energize for our next encounters. Given how busy our lives are, finding adequate time to do this can be tough. So for those of you who find yourself interacting with an introvert who seems a bit out of sorts, it may very well be that we have not been able to sufficiently recharge our batteries.

9. **Introverts do not like being the center of attention, particularly in social settings.** Again it is an energy thing. Being the center of attention at a social event requires a lot of energy and takes us introverts outside of our comfort zone. While we are able to do what it takes and can actually be quite outgoing and engaging while doing it, introverts need to find some quiet time soon thereafter to recharge.

10. **Introverts are self-aware and know we are introverted.** Sometimes introverts feel insecure or even guilty about being the way we are. This is particularly true given the societal pressure to always be on, which tends to make things even more difficult for the introverts among us. We usually know what we need to do in order to get ourselves back into equilibrium if we have been engaging in extroverted activities. The extroverts among us should do what they can to give us the space to do that, knowing that we will be back with them all the more quickly.

It is of paramount importance for us to consider these qualities and predilections in the context of our careers and how we must perform, so that we can excel in a profession that has been and continues to undergo profound change - and which seems much better suited to the extroverts among us. We all need to embrace who we are and to understand our natural tendencies. Whether an introvert or an extrovert, there is no right or wrong - we are wired a certain way and we need to acknowledge and accept this about ourselves.

The introverts among us should understand that our natural tendencies can sometimes lead to self-limiting behaviors and that sometimes we need to turn it off. This is particularly true with respect to the more extroverted activities associated with networking, business development and building your personal brand. Getting to know potential business leads is an uphill battle if you do not put yourself out there. If people do not know who you are and what you have to offer; then it becomes challenging to develop the relationships, credibility and trust that are crucial to developing a business or practice. These types of situations can be quite difficult for introverts. Nevertheless, when we find ourselves in situations calling for us to be more extroverted, we need to get out of our heads and into the moment. We all need to develop a comfort zone for being outside of our comfort zone. If we are passionate about what we do, we will naturally project it and want to share it with others, regardless of whether we are introverts or extroverts.

Collaboration is an important part of the problem-solving and client service process. This can often be more difficult for introverts who, as noted above, generally prefer to work by themselves to minimize interactions with others. As professionals, we need to understand that this can often lead to a less-than-optimal result, both in the work product we deliver to clients as well as in the perceptions of our coworkers, who may not fully understand the introvert's behaviors and tendencies in these types of situations. We must all make a concerted effort to balance the benefits of different types of working styles and contributions and work together to reach optimal results for our clients.

Introverts can and often do rise to leadership positions. A number of authors, including Cain and Jim Collins in his landmark management book, *Good to Great,* have studied effective leadership qualities, many of which are attributable to introverts. These skills include strong listening and intuition, introspection, deep thinking, humility and compassion. If we each look at the leaders in our organizations, communities and globally, we are sure to find at least a few introverts among them.

Whether an introvert or an extrovert, each of us is an interesting amalgam of contradictions and I invite you to explore both the yin and the yang within yourself.

Going Global

Law Firms and Legal Departments as Global Organizations

Both law firms and legal departments are invaluable partners in addressing legal and business issues. Even if a business' operations are primarily domestic in scope, given the global nature of the economy, the marketplace, politics and technological interconnectivity, every business has a ripple effect on others, and vice versa. It is inevitable that customers, legal and business issues, and problem-solving processes and solutions, each have an international reach.

We live in a global economy. This means that all businesses and their lawyers must be where their clients are, both substantively and geographically, and able to think multi-nationally, even if the business only operates locally.

The Challenges of Being a Global Organization

One of the biggest challenges is in striking a delicate balance among a variety of competing interests, all of which are important to the long-term success of an organization. This includes reaching an optimal solution to the legal and business issues which arise, particularly where the consequences are international in scope. It is also a challenge to stay current, relevant and competitive in each of the financial centers across the world. Seamless and open communication with your team members and clients across the globe is vital. You must also be proactive, forward-thinking, innovative and a leader, rather than being reactive and a follower.

Another major challenge is knowing the laws, customs and culture of other countries in which you are doing business. Culture impacts business, and you must be able to negotiate and bridge any differences successfully in order to have a global practice. These challenges include navigating language and time zone differences, as well as any differences in problem-solving approaches and deal and negotiation cadences.

The Necessary Skills to Go Global

Lawyers with a successful global practice are, first and foremost, great substantive lawyers with a strong business sense and excellent interpersonal skills. They are open-minded and able to appreciate legal and business issues from a variety of angles. They also have a working understanding and sensitivity to other cultures, customs and perspectives. To the extent that there is a knowledge gap, they are willing to learn through work projects, and they also study, travel and seek advice from others with such experience. In addition, they are collaborative, a team player and have an understanding that legal and business decisions in today's global environment will often have a ripple effect beyond the matter at hand, and analyze issues from that perspective as well.

Flexibility and patience are also important. You cannot be too set in your ways, because your counterpart across the globe likely sees things differently. You need to compromise to accomplish your goals. Be mindful of your limitations and retain experienced counsel to help you navigate those areas in which you may not have the requisite skills or knowledge. While you can always learn technical details and applicable law, working successfully with people from different countries, cultures and world views requires a skillset that is as much people-oriented as it is substantive.

LEADERSHIP

Leadership is not about being the loudest person in the room, barking orders or expecting blind obedience from every member of your team. That is not leadership. That is dictatorship. Dictatorship lacks strategic thinking and foresight and is ineffective in the long run. Leadership, on the other hand, is intentional and courageous and, when done right, changes businesses and lives.

The truth is, anyone can play the role of a dictator, clutching power, hoarding credit and using fear as a means of control. But real leadership? That takes courage, consistency and a deep sense of responsibility for the people you serve.

A strong leader does not dominate; they elevate. They do not micromanage; they trust. They do not operate from ego; they act from vision, purpose and a genuine desire to help others succeed.

You can feel the difference when you are around a true leader. People want to follow them, not because they have to, but because they believe in the leader's vision. They feel seen, supported, valued and challenged in the best ways.

Dictators command. Leaders inspire.

Leadership Is not About You—But It Starts with You

To lead well, you must first be committed to growth - your own and everyone else's. That means taking responsibility for your blind spots. It also means learning from failure and continuously investing in building your leadership skills, because no matter how long you have been at it, there is always room for improvement. Being a great leader is not about perfection. It is about presence, purpose and a willingness to grow.

You become a better leader by putting in the work. That can be by reading books written by other great leaders, taking workshops and actively engaging in real-world situations that test your patience, communication skills and resilience. The best leaders have battle scars. They have made mistakes, gotten things wrong and learned what not to do just as often as they have learned what to do.

In one of Christina's earliest leadership roles, she quickly realized that while she appreciated the valuable advice passed down from her predecessors, the only sure way to understand the responsibility of leading others was by figuring things out for herself. *"I had to find my own voice, learn how to navigate conflict, and discover how to lead without trying to control every outcome in ways that felt authentic for me."* That is another thing about great leaders: they understand that there is no one-size-fits-all solution for every situation, and at the end of the day, there is no substitute for showing up and doing the hard work yourself.

Real Leaders Do Not Just Lead Work—They Lead People

Being an expert in your craft matters. A great leader knows what success looks like in their industry and how to navigate the internal dynamics of their organization. But just as critical as technical know-how is the ability to understand people. (There is that EQ again!)

Leadership is about creating and navigating relationships. It requires empathy, the ability to listen deeply, and having the selflessness to put others' needs ahead of your own. It is not about being the most intelligent person in the room. It is about helping others be their best and smartest selves. It is about building a team of people who feel confident, capable and empowered because of your influence, not in spite of it.

Dictators hoard the spotlight. Leaders share it. They give credit generously and surround themselves with other strong, capable people, many of whom could one day succeed them. They are not threatened by that, and in fact, they welcome it.

Strong leaders strive to raise others up, while dictators try to push others down.

Resistance is Not Rebellion

One of the most important things you must accept as a leader is that not everyone will like you.

You can lead with honesty, vision and heart, but still encounter resistance. That does not mean you are failing as a leader. It simply means you are doing something that matters.

Often, the most substantial resistance comes from those most afraid of change. They may have been burned by bad leadership in the past, have their own agenda, feel threatened or simply be stuck in their ways. Your job is not to win them over with charm or to force them into submission; it is to understand where they are coming from, communicate clearly and keep leading despite their resistance or hesitation.

It is usually not personal. It is fear, insecurity or misunderstanding. And sometimes, the most powerful thing you can do as a leader is to meet that resistance with curiosity and compassion rather than defensiveness.

When people feel heard, they soften. And when they feel valued, they show up.

If You Want to Lead, Do Not Wait for Permission

You do not need a title to be a leader. Leadership can start anywhere: on a project team, in a volunteer role, on a committee, or in your community. The key is to take initiative and act with integrity.

Some of the most powerful leadership lessons come from these small moments, when you take the lead on a task, guide a discussion, support a colleague or rally people around a shared goal. These are the places where you build your confidence, practice your voice and shape your own unique leadership style.

If you are in a place that does not offer growth opportunities, do not wait for a promotion that may never come. Instead, create your own path. This might mean deciding to move to a different department or even a new organization. It is imperative that you do not give up on your goals just because someone else is not able to see your full potential.

Great leaders are not handed power. They earn and seize it through consistent action, service and growth.

Strong Leaders Build Strong Cultures

You can often tell when a team has a strong leader. There is a sense of energy, clarity and momentum. People enjoy their work, and they collaborate, communicate and celebrate each other's wins. They all row in the same direction because they believe in the shared vision and their leader.

You can also tell when a team is under weak leadership. Morale is low, people keep their heads down, turnover is high and creativity is absent. The strongest talent often leaves first because great employees will not stick around under poor leadership for long.

Weak leaders stifle innovation, dismiss input, take credit, place blame and avoid accountability. Dictatorship creates disengagement and burnout because no one thrives in an environment where they feel micromanaged, overlooked or undervalued.

On the other hand, strong leaders empower. They listen. They guide. They create a culture where people want to show up and do their best. Not because they are afraid, but because they are inspired.

Leadership Is a Long Game

You do not become a great leader overnight, and you do not stop growing once you get there. Leadership is a continuous process of learning, growing and adapting. It takes vision, resilience and the humility to ask for help, to admit when you are wrong and to continue striving, not for personal glory but for collective success.

Strong leadership is about being nimble and versatile, not rigid or reactive. It is about seeing around the corner - the long game, where the organization is headed, what employees need in order to thrive, and how to best shape a future that is bigger than one person's ambition.

You cannot fake good leadership. People know when it is real, and they feel it in how they are treated, how they are heard and how they are led through both triumphs and challenges.

If you are ready to step into your leadership potential, remember this: You do not need to have all the answers. You simply need to care deeply, act with integrity, and keep showing up. Leadership is not about telling people what to do. It is about showing them what is possible.

SUCCESS IS NEVER A ONE-PERSON SHOW

In the early days of our careers, we often think of excellence as a solo act. We pour everything we have into developing our skills, growing our professional knowledge base, and delivering the highest-quality work possible. While those things do matter, they are never the whole picture. It is not until we experience the undeniable momentum that comes from being part of a high-performing team that we realize how much we lack by trying to go it alone. As it turns out, success is never a one-person show - it is a collaborative performance where every player counts.

Collaboration > Individual Achievement

We accomplish exponentially more when we work in tandem with others, not just around them. Many clients and customers might initially be drawn to a specific individual or professional, but their staying power - the reason they return and refer us to others - is often inextricably linked to the team that we create around us. In a high-stakes environment, assembling the right group of people can make or break the outcome.

But great teams do not come together by accident.

High-performing teams are built intentionally, with foresight, self-awareness and emotional intelligence. When they come together, they are more than a group of talented individuals; they are a well-balanced ecosystem where the right mix of skills, communication styles and personalities is aligned to support a shared purpose.

Knowing the People Behind the Performance

Being a strong team player and leader starts with awareness of others and yourself. It requires more than simply knowing someone's job title; it demands an understanding of each team member's unique strengths, areas for improvement, and how they perform both individually and within a group dynamic. A few questions you can ask yourself when creating a high-performing team are:

- Who handles high-pressure moments with grace and ease?

- Who brings creative out-of-the-box solutions when everyone else hits a brick wall?

- Who acts as a quiet anchor to help keep the team and projects grounded?

Effective team leaders (and team members) know when it is time to tag someone in, for what purpose, and how to structure their involvement. Sometimes that means staggering the participation of team members and being mindful of maintaining a balance of personality and energy. Too much of any particular trait is generally not a good thing.

Setting clear roles and expectations is also essential to the performance of a team. When people do not know what is expected of them, it creates friction, insecurity and inefficiency. Transparency is not optional - it is foundational.

The Human Side of Teamwork

No matter how sophisticated the work or how specialized the skills, every high-performing team boils down to one essential component: its people.

People need connection. That means actually talking to one another, not just exchanging emails or direct messages online. As much as we do not want to at times, it is important that we pick up the phone or schedule a face-to-face meeting and check in with our teammates with a moment or two of casual conversation. These human moments build trust and camaraderie among a team. They signal *"We are in this together,"* and that sense of shared ownership is one of the strongest drivers of consistent high performance.

When teammates trust each other, they speak up. They feel comfortable sharing new ideas, voicing concerns and, at times, even disagreeing with the current status quo. As the leader of a high-performing team, it is important to remember that healthy disagreements are a part of the process. Civil, respectful debates about how to best approach a challenge can often lead to better, more creative solutions than any one person could have reached alone. This is where learning happens, bonds are formed and performance excels.

Dynamic, Not Static

High-performing teams are never static. They evolve in real time as people, businesses and client needs evolve. The team that was right last year will likely need to make changes this year, and that is not a sign of failure. It is a sign of responsiveness and evolution.

The most successful teams are built not only around tasks but also around alignment with clients, customers and shared outcomes. It is not about checking boxes; it is about creating synergy. The right mix of skills, styles and mindsets allows high-performing teams to respond quickly and effectively across diverse challenges and opportunities.

Diversity in thought, experience and approach is not just a buzzword. It is a competitive advantage.

Egos Down, Standards Up

High-performing teams are defined by their commitment to a collective standard of excellence. Their focus is not on individual accolades, but on shared successes. That means checking egos at the door and staying aligned with the ultimate goal.

Communication is constant, collaboration is expected and everyone is held accountable, not only for *what* they contribute, but for *how* they contribute. The best teams do not tolerate toxicity or neglect. They hold one another to high standards because they care about each other and the mission. And when it all clicks, it can be transformative.

Leadership Within the Team

Whether you are the official leader or not, your ability to be a valuable teammate matters greatly. A strong team lifts everyone, giving each member the space to grow, lead and evolve. Within a team, it is important to remember that leadership does not mean dominance. It means discernment, knowing when to speak up, when to step back, when to guide, and when to follow.

Strong emotional intelligence is the unspoken currency of high-performing teams. It helps you read the room, anticipate needs and navigate dynamics gracefully. It also helps to build credibility with new team members and maintain harmony during transitions. If you want to lead well, you must start by teaming well.

It's Not Just About Work

Here is the real kicker: when you learn how to be a strong teammate in your professional life, it spills into every other area, including your relationships, your family and your community. You become a better listener, communicate more clearly and offer support without feeling the need to take the spotlight or center stage. Being part of a high-performing team also changes how you move through the world. It teaches you that shared goals build stronger results and more meaningful connections. That trust is built over time and reinforced through small, consistent actions. People matter and ultimately, the best work - the kind that matters - never happens in a vacuum.

Wellness is a Leadership Tool, Not a Luxury

No matter what industry you are in or what position you hold, the pace of modern business is constant and unrelenting. There is underlying pressure in every inbox notification, meeting and project, urging us to work harder, scale faster and stay ahead of the competition. If you pause even for a moment, you risk falling behind. Too often, stress is not a side effect of our high-speed world - it is a constant companion.

But here is the hard truth: *if we do not devote time to learning how to manage our stress better, it will manage us.* And the longer we ignore it, the more likely it is to quietly unravel everything we have worked so hard to build: our businesses, our relationships, our health, and ourselves.

The Cost of Carrying On

Not so long ago, a steady stream of work seemed to fall from the sky, and all you needed to do was to simply show up and do your job well. But now, that game has changed. You are expected to satisfy existing clients while simultaneously chasing new ones, stay visible in shrinking markets, and reinvent yourself in professions that seem to constantly redefine "normal." This is just not sustainable without strong internal support, which is inextricably linked to your mental wellness, emotional bandwidth, and ability to maintain clarity and resilience under pressure.

We are not robots, built to function at a breakneck pace without rest, direction and purpose. We are human, and when stress runs the show, mistakes happen. Communication slips, expectations get lost in translation, relationships get strained and our overall performance takes a hit, not because we are being lazy, but because we are physically, mentally and emotionally depleted.

Repair. Reflect. Reframe.

When your performance falls short, it is generally a sign that it is time to slow down, take a step back and deconstruct the situation to figure out a better way. Ask yourself: Where did the misstep occur? Was it a communication gap? Was there a lack of clarity on the scope of support or who owns the project? A case of imminent mental burnout? A misalignment of priorities? Or were you simply overwhelmed and out of alignment with yourself?

Taking the time to unpack these events is not just about doing damage control but honing your personal leadership skills. As professionals, we are responsible for owning our mistakes, fixing what we can, thinking it through on our own or with a trusted confidante, and tuning into what our body and mind are trying to tell us.

The Mental Health Equation

As professionals, we often pride ourselves on our stamina, pushing through late nights, juggling impending deadlines, and showing up polished even when we are running on fumes. But this hustle-at-all-costs mindset is not sustainable. Over time, the body rebels, the mind falters and the spirit dims. We owe it to ourselves to remember that wellness is not a luxury; it is a leadership tool.

It is not just about going to the gym more or changing our diet. True wellness means finding harmony across all dimensions of our lives - the physical, mental, emotional and spiritual. It means learning to listen *inward,* even when the world demands that you keep looking *outward*.

You do not need to become a wellness guru overnight, but you do need to get honest about what fuels you and what drains you. For Christina, being fueled comes in many forms, notably daily meditation, journaling, exercise and laughter. For David, transcendental meditation, listening to a Bruce Springsteen or Stevie Wonder album, riding the Peloton, and spending time with pets helps him recharge.

Wellness is a lifelong practice that is personal and unique to each individual. There is no one-size-fits-all solution. But there *is* a universal truth at the root: when you feel like yourself, you optimize your performance.

The Warning Signs

The quickest way to know that something is off is when life begins feeling heavy. You may find falling and staying asleep more difficult, with the meager rest you get being filled with dreams revolving around your inbox, client meetings and urgent deadlines. The single cup of coffee you enjoy each morning may turn into 3, 4 or even 5, becoming a crutch instead of a treat. You may have a shorter fuse, and find yourself snapping at others. These are signs that your body is waving a white flag and needing attention.

On the flip side? You know you are in the flow when your thoughts are clear, your energy is up and your creativity feels alive. When your mind is not racing, and you are able to focus with ease. When you feel present. Empowered. Whole.

Which version of you is the one your team, your clients and your loved ones want and need?

Rest Is Not a Reward

This is worth repeating: Rest is not a reward for productivity. It is a prerequisite.

We must stop treating self-care like a weekend indulgence. Taking care of your mind and body is not selfish; it is strategic and helps you to stay focused, creative, collaborative and compassionate towards yourself and others.

When you are mentally, emotionally and physically well-rested, your patience returns, your vision expands, and your ability to lead, inspire and innovate is amplified. You go from just checking boxes to knowing that you are making a real impact on the world and the lives of those around you.

So, ask yourself: Are you creating space for recovery in your routine? Or are you simply waiting for a crash before you give yourself permission to pause?

Saying "No" Is a Power Move

One of the biggest myths among professionals is that saying *yes* to everything makes you indispensable. In fact, the opposite is true. It makes you distracted, less intentional and on the fast track to burnout. Learning to say *no* with grace, clarity and resolve is one of the most powerful tools in your wellness arsenal. It protects your time, energy and health, allowing you to better focus on what truly matters.

Giving yourself permission to say *no* to things that feel less aligned, carry a sense of false urgency or require people-pleasing at the expense of your well-being is the quickest way to say *yes* to your physical, emotional and mental health, and to your own bigger purpose.

Our Five Focus To-Dos

In today's world, we must bring mindful focus back into our lives to not just survive, but to thrive. These reminders help anchor us when stress starts creeping in:

1. **Focus on what you love.**
   Let joy be your compass. When you lead from passion instead of pressure, you will be more energized, creative and effective.

2. **Focus on what really matters.**
   Do not confuse urgency with importance. Be discerning about what actually deserves your energy.

3. **Focus on the positive.**
   Gratitude and positivity are not fluff; they are fuel. They build resilience and deepen relationships.

4. **Focus on being your best.**
   Keep growing and learning. Show up for yourself so that you can show up for others.

5. **Focus on the well-being of others.**
   Empathy is not only human, it is strategic. Strong teams and client relationships start with compassion.

If you take nothing else from this chapter, take this: *your well-being is not separate from your success—it is the foundation of it.* The most impactful professionals are not the ones who sacrifice everything for their careers. Rather, they are the ones who understand that their energy, clarity and emotional health are their greatest assets. They lead with intention, modeling the ability to pause when needed, and creating space for their team to experience reflection, recovery and joy. Remember, resting, and asking for and being open to receiving support, are not weaknesses - they are the signs of wisdom and of a strong leader.

Navigating Uncertainty

While the topic of navigating uncertainty is one that many of us have experienced in one way or another, it became a serious issue affecting the entire world in early 2020 with the COVID-19 pandemic, lockdown, and shelter-in-place orders across the country.

Uncertainty in the Workplace

Uncertainty is not clearly defined, and can relate to any number of things. Uncertainty comes in all forms. It can mean a lack of confidence. Will I get this job? Will I win this contract or a new client account? Is the advice I gave my client correct? Will there be a recession this year? If my company is acquired, will I still have a job? It can also be a lack of certainty in the future of the global economy, politics and business, whether for the short-, medium- or long-term. This impacts the viability of businesses and drives decisions intended to help safeguard their future to the extent possible. Professionals must watch these trends closely to predict what clients are likely to need, and how uncertainty is likely to impact their own clientele.

From Christina's perspective:

"As a partner in a law firm, each year I develop a business plan for my practice and forecast projected billings for my clients. These estimates are based mostly on the pipeline of projects I have for each client and prospective client as well as what the year is projected to look like for their respective businesses. Prognosticating as to whether clients are on an upward trend or likely to have a slower year, and knowing what their

pressure points tend to be, are important factors in bringing more certainty into a situation which can otherwise be tough to predict. On a bigger scale, other partners likewise make these projections for clients, and firms take these estimates into account on an aggregate basis in determining estimated collections for the year. In times where business growth is more uncertain, firms are more conservative in their business expenses and projected budgets which will, in turn, impact targets for hiring, staff salaries, decisions on whether to enter new markets and the like."

From David's perspective:

"My job is all about planning for uncertainty. In law and in business, little is certain; outcomes are rarely known beyond doubt. As in-house counsel, my job is risk management. Risk is born out of uncertainty. My role is to help identify the risks my organization is exposed to and help the business leaders plan accordingly. I start with the legal risks and, working with my business colleagues, help identify the business risks and then together we create plans to manage them. We often have the opportunity to be on the forefront of educating our business colleagues about upcoming uncertainty/risk and help lead the charge to prepare for it."

The Upside of Uncertainty

Uncertainty generally comes with flux and movement, both of which indicate that circumstances are dynamic, and not static. This can bring great opportunity - to grow, stretch, do different things, and to do the same things differently - and better. Sometimes it is hard to see the other side of uncertainty in the moment, but these windows to improve and evolve rarely, if ever, come with just maintaining the status quo.

Uncertainty keeps you on your toes, so that you are better prepared and suffer less disruption in your business, work and life when things go differently than expected. If you have given thought to the possibility of things going sideways, you are prepared, and it is less disruptive and chaotic. We both often say that we have developed a comfort zone of being outside of our comfort zone. David explains, *"I do not know what novel issues will next land on my desk, but I do know that they inevitably will. When they do, I take a deep breath and dive in to figure them out - sometimes it is scary to have so much uncertainty but I have learned to embrace it and use it, to improve and evolve, both for myself and for my company."*

Uncertainty and Resilience Through the COVID-19 Pandemic

The global pandemic and the resulting stay-at-home orders drastically impacted both work and home life for us all. The good news is that many organizations were prepared for this scenario, technologically and otherwise. In many ways, it was business day-to-day, other than the fact that we did not connect with people in person. Video conferencing was a tremendous help in staying connected in a more meaningful way than either on the phone or by email. However, when we stopped working and looked at what was going on around us, there was a profound shift in the world, and this significantly impacted our clients - both as professionals and as people, as well as our businesses. None of us will be the same.

Working at home was the most tangible change for many. The intentionality of our adaptability increased exponentially thereafter. For many who are in positions that require them to be highly collaborative, being in constant communication is imperative to the success of the individual and the team as a whole. One of the toughest difficulties that came with this change was the issue of separating our work and personal lives.

From Christina's perspective:

"Going into the COVID-19 lockdown situation, I had these great visions of having more time to exercise, rest, take care of chores around my house and other tasks. What I found is that I had greater difficulty separating my work from my personal life. I found myself working longer

hours than I had before, not having any downtime and not accomplishing any of the personal goals I had set for myself. It was only once I became more mindful of this issue, that I was able to reaffirm my intent to better create separation so that I could get at least a little bit more rest and clear my head."

From David's perspective:

"As someone who was used to working at home only a few days a year, it was difficult, shifting to working from home full-time. There was no concern with having enough work to do or the motivation to do it; the concern was how to stop working and maintain some semblance of a personal/non-work life. What had been my commute time was added to my work time. I was at my dining room table at 6:00 a.m., working non-stop for the next 12 to 14 hours. I started wearing my regular office attire during the day and changing clothes in the evening as if I were coming home from the office, which helped make a difference in mindset in terms of delineating between work and personal time. I will also say that my dry cleaner was quite happy to see me that first Saturday after I made the change.

My company has multiple business units across the US and in other countries. Even before the pandemic, I was used to working with clients remotely. We have always connected by telephone, email and text, with in-person meetings typically only once or twice a year. When the pandemic started, those communication styles continued with video conferences. The real difference was the quarantine state of mind. In many respects, that isolation can seem greater even if, in fact, we have always worked together remotely from each other. The biggest difference in the way I now stay connected with colleagues and team members is that we check in personally more often, beyond strictly talking business."

The irony about the pandemic lockdown was that while we were all required to exercise social distancing, we as a society were more resourceful in finding ways to both stay close and actually grow closer. We quickly found that little acts of kindness, no matter what they were, would go a long way. This still holds true today, even after life has returned to "normal." Whether it is a quick check-in call, emailing someone to say that you are thinking about them, or having a virtual coffee with a client by video, all of these gestures carry new meaning.

Professionals in a wide range of industries have proven just how resilient and innovative they can be. Networking and relationship building is more important than ever, as individuals seek to reconnect with new and existing clients, colleagues, and referral sources. The good news is we are all in the same boat. The concept of virtual networking is something we are all doing together; it simply has to be accepted as the way to do it. Networking in this new normal is accomplished to a large degree in the same way we have always connected, but we must be intentional about it. Video conferencing is the best way to virtually network, especially with people you are just meeting and getting to know.

With many businesses still choosing to work remotely, even if only part-time, it is important for the lines of communication to remain open for high-performing teams to be successful. Team leads need to regularly assess individual and collective performance across financial and productivity levers, and should have regular meetings to discuss what is working well and where the challenges lie. It is also important for teams to be nimble, resilient and creative in their approach to getting the job done. Patience, understanding and compassion are critical in shifting the mindset from a short-term phenomenon to a longer-term reality.

Although video conferencing is hugely beneficial, there is still something that gets lost by not being together. Many organizations have recognized that this interpersonal glue helps ensure that the workplace culture remains healthy and is a driving force in attracting and retaining talent, thus bringing the majority of their workforce back into the office. There are often efficiencies with resources and technology that may exist in the workplace that do not exist remotely. Being back in the office with your colleagues also makes work more fun and helps alleviate the monotony of being at home.

Deciding how to best strike that balance between in office and from home depends on numerous factors, including who you are, where you work and the level of flexibility in your job. It also matters whether your preference is in alignment with your employer's choices. Christina explains, *"I work at a firm where we have adopted a hybrid approach, and my preference is in alignment with that model. I am an introvert, and while some have called COVID-19 an introvert's dream, I could not work 100% remotely without losing significant elements of my job that I love. The most important is being with people and connecting in person."*

From Christina's perspective:

"When I look back on my career as an associate, there were so many mentoring opportunities I got by virtue of being in my office when a partner happened to walk by with a project they needed help on. There were countless opportunities to develop both professional and personal relationships with my colleagues by virtue of being in the office together, whether by grabbing lunch, coffee or a drink. This would happen spontaneously rather than being scheduled. I do not think I would be where I am today as an attorney and professional if I did not have these opportunities.

Speaking from personal experience, returning to the office was a combination of joy, anticipation, apprehension and sadness for me. Anticipation and joy to see people that I care deeply about and had not seen in a long time. Apprehension because like everyone else, I was concerned about getting COVID-19, and about the possibility of giving it to someone else. Sadness because so much time had passed since we were all last together and things were more normal. Also, because so much had changed for all of us. We all know people who got sick or passed away during the pandemic. Some of them were people with whom we worked closely. The sense that nothing will ever be the same again can be sobering, but is counterbalanced by the happiness of being together again."

From David's perspective:

"For lawyers, especially younger lawyers, associates, and in-house attorneys, it is critical to work in the office a few days a week. For those in their first several years of practice, it is essential to be in the office with more senior attorneys. It is incumbent upon those senior attorneys to help train the next generation. Yes, there is much we can do just as well remotely as in the office. However, there is no substitute for what we can learn simply by being in the same room. Learning how to conduct yourself in different settings requires doing so in person to truly master it. You cannot overstate the value of simply being present to get access to new opportunities. Oftentimes, a senior lawyer or business leader needs help at that moment and will grab someone who is physically near them. You miss those opportunities when you are not in the office, and those ultimately are the drivers of closer relationships and career advancement. Watching other associates in action, and being in meetings and negotiations in person, is how you learn. You get to see how more experienced professionals work. You can see how they conduct themselves in a variety of situations. You cannot get the body language or nuance that underlies the words being spoken through a computer screen. Being live and in person with others is how you best learn to be a professional.

At first, returning to the office after so many months away was quite scary. It was fatiguing and disorienting. However, we moved past that fairly quickly as we got used to going back and being around other people. Yes, many of us developed a fondness for being at home, but do not underestimate the negative impacts of loneliness that you may not be aware of when you are only at home. Also, remember to consciously practice patience and kindness with everyone, not only your colleagues, but also people outside of work who may have had a rough time. A little kindness goes a long way."

While the pandemic left an indelible mark on each aspect of our lives, there has been some good that has emerged. Making it through the pandemic has been empowering and put circumstances that pre-pandemic we viewed as tough into a whole different perspective. It is inevitable that our frames of reference have changed compared to what our day-to-day existence was before and during the pandemic, and we have become more resilient in the process. The struggles we have been forced to overcome - and the losses so many of us have experienced - have taught us the importance of gratitude for each day we are given to make a difference in this world.

Recommendations For When You are Faced with Uncertainty

When your circumstances are causing you to feel uncertain as to how best to move forward, shift your perspective, reframe your approach and plan accordingly. Remember that it is a marathon, not a sprint; be innovative and try several approaches to see which are the most successful and adjust. Regularly assess what is most effective and most challenging for you, what leads to the most successful results and address whatever issues there are in real time. To the extent you need assistance from others to handle these challenges, do not be shy about seeking help.

Remember we are all learning as we go. We all have challenging circumstances to navigate, so be patient with others and be understanding. Be open to change in ways you may not have been previously, and embrace the inevitable as opportunities to reinvent yourself and your approach. Now is a great time to try out something new.

Role Models, Confidantes and the Power of Mutual Trust

There are turning points in life that do not come from *what* we know but from *who* we know. No matter how smart, strategic or self-aware we are, we all need people who can reflect our best back to us, ask provocative questions, and offer hard truths with soft hearts. We need role models to show us what is possible, and confidantes to help us navigate what is real.

From the outside, success might look like a solo endeavor - a person leading boldly, making decisions and forging a path. But inside every truly transformative story, you will find a small constellation of people who gave you permission, perspective and presence when it mattered most.

This chapter is about those people, and about becoming that person for others.

What Makes a Good Role Model

Role models are not necessarily people we know personally, but they show us the kind of person we want to be. They embody qualities we admire and aspire to, and lead not only through excellence in their craft, but also through how they carry themselves and treat others.

A good role model leads with honesty, integrity and professionalism in business, leadership and life. This includes not only excellent decision-making skills and professional acumen, but also who they are when no one is watching. It is how they handle losses, own their mistakes and stand up for others, who may not have the power or confidence we do.

These people *do the right thing* - not for recognition, but because it is who they are.

Great role models do not just excel individually but also *invest in others.* They give back, mentor, open doors, advocate for justice, and leave communities and individuals stronger than they found them. The best role models are not selfish and do not hoard the spotlight. Instead, they make a point of bringing others along, and understand that professional success means little if it does not also lift someone else up in the process.

A good sense of humor helps as well. Taking their *work* seriously does not mean they have to take *themselves* too seriously. Humor provides a way for individuals to connect, eases tension and invites people to bring their whole selves into a space. A role model who can make you laugh while modeling strength and wisdom is someone worth paying attention to.

From Christina's perspective:

"My mother, who passed away when I was a senior in high school, was very much an inspiration to me. She was born and raised in Mexico City and was incredibly intelligent and well-educated. She taught me the importance of dreaming big, believing in and making something of myself and going out into the world and having the courage to do that. Even to this day, she is still an incredible influence on me and really inspired me to be the person I am today.

Another important role model for me is Mark Feldman, who is a retired partner from my first law firm. I worked with him for nearly 25 years. He is a brilliant lawyer and internationally renowned in the IP field, and he took me as a very young 23-year-old attorney fresh out of law school and inspired me to get very excited about the law. He helped me develop both professionally and personally into the person I am today. I know that I would not be where I am today if it were not for him. And it is because of his leadership, as well as his generosity in taking me under his wing and spending the time that he spent with me, that I am the well-rounded professional I am today.

Another person who has been an important influence on me is a friend and colleague at my first firm who passed away in 2004 - her name was Kathy Nooney. She was a devoted wife and mother, and an exceptional lawyer who was very dedicated to pro bono and was all about making a difference to everyone around her and serving people. Her life purpose was public service. Even with everything she had going on in her life she was very humble and generous. Those are all qualities that are important to carry forward into your career and your life."

From David's perspective:

"My primary role model is my father, who was also an attorney. He was the consummate professional. He always conducted himself and treated others with honesty, integrity and professionalism. He treated everybody equally; it did not matter who they were, what their job was, race or gender, or economic status. He also taught me the true meaning of professionalism, that we, as lawyers, owe society a duty to conduct ourselves with honesty, integrity and professionalism. He also taught me the value of fighting for the underdog and how to be a generous leader.

Another role model is my mother. She was a schoolteacher, but she called herself a professional volunteer because she was on so many non-profit boards. She strongly influenced my life, especially with regard to volunteerism. I have been on nonprofit boards and engaged in other volunteer activities both inside and outside the legal profession since I graduated from law school.

Several of my role models and mentors are my contemporaries, people I admire and who inspire me to remain true to myself, my goals and my principles. Some are actually younger than me, which I mention because role models and mentors are not only people who are your elders. They include my friend Jason Brown, who inspires me to strive to be the best I can be and to always approach life with excitement and laughter. Also, my friend Dan Harper, who reminds me of the value of critical thinking and of rational discourse.

Finally, I want to add my wife, because she inspires me and reminds me of the importance of remaining true to my core values, acting with integrity and to being open to growth and improvement."

The Quiet Power of Confidantes

While role models show us what to strive for, confidantes help us navigate the process. A confidante is more than a trusted advisor. They are someone who has earned the right to hear the things we do not often say out loud to anyone else - the late-night doubts, the half-formed decisions and the "What if I'm wrong?" moments. A confidante is both a sounding board and a soft landing, someone who knows your values and will hold you accountable, even when you may drift off course.

Unlike mentors or sponsors, a confidante usually walks beside you, not ahead of you. The relationship is mutual, and it evolves over time through years of nurturing, along with shared values. A confidante knows when to speak, when to simply listen and how to hold space for your truth.

What a Confidante Is and Is Not

A confidante is someone you admire both professionally and personally, and that you can trust so deeply that you can bring them your most delicate decisions and complicated emotions without fear of judgment or betrayal. That relationship can be reciprocal, meaning you can offer the same level of presence and trust in return. These relationships do not form quickly; they tend to grow and evolve over time. It can be helpful to observe how someone moves through the world, handles pressure and treats people when there is no upside for them. If you feel a connection rooted in shared integrity and intellect, you can choose to foster the relationship.

You do not need to share everything with every confidante for it to be valuable. Indeed, some conversations are best had with your spouse, partner or friends. In all cases, remain mindful that sharing a sensitive matter might unintentionally compromise that person or put them in a difficult

position. When you see the potential for a conflict of interest or an uncomfortable situation, do your best to choose discretion. Being discerning does not make a relationship less real; it makes it more respectful.

Why Both Matter

You do not need a hundred role models or a large team of confidantes, but you *do* need a few people who make you feel confident in who you are and help you remember your values when life gets challenging. We move differently through the world when we have people to look up to and talk with. We lead better and make choices not just with strategy, but with integrity, soul and passion.

These relationships are the antidote to the isolation that so often accompanies ambition. They are the bridge between where we are and where we want to be, not because someone else is pulling us along, but because they believe we can get there. The people we look up to show us what is possible, and those we confide in remind us of what matters. When we can become those people for others, we do not just change our own lives - we help shift the landscape of leadership, community and connection for generations to come.

Pro Bono, Volunteering and Extracurriculars

Now more than ever, there is a collective realization that giving back is not just "the right thing to do"—it is also a powerful tool for personal, professional and community transformation. These efforts stretch beyond charity—they are acts of leadership, humanity and legacy. There are more individuals and organizations than ever before with legal needs for which they are unable to pay. Sometimes it is truly a matter of life or death. There is also increased awareness that these needs are both local and global, and there are many ways for US-based lawyers to meaningfully assist people abroad. This has led to more flexibility with pro bono and a real willingness to engage in creative and collaborative partnerships with clients, potential clients, trade associations, governments and various other organizations, both within and outside the US, and this has opened the doors to pro bono opportunities and volunteering that did not exist before.

Pro bono work has always been an important part of the profession and the professional requirements for practicing lawyers. Over the years, there have been some very creative initiatives and a greater push to get more attorneys involved in pro bono work, both in law firms and in the in-house world. Law firms and in-house departments have been launching various cooperative partnerships in which both in-house and private practice lawyers work together to provide pro bono services. This includes staffing legal aid clinics and forming creative partnerships with nonlegal organizations, such as legal-medical partnerships in which lawyers and hospitals team up to provide pro bono help to families and individuals trying to navigate issues such as Medicaid and its maze of paperwork.

Remember that civic service is about service to others, not to promote yourself. Pro bono work, volunteering and board service are a means of giving back to your community, not to pad your resume.

Finding Quality Pro Bono Opportunities

There are endless opportunities for everyone to make a meaningful difference with pro bono, regardless of their practice area and years of experience. So many firms, corporations, bar associations, nonprofit organizations and other entities have or are in the process of institutionalizing pro bono programs with a myriad of litigation and transactional opportunities. Unfortunately, there is never a shortage of these needs, and it is just a matter of going out and finding them if they do not typically cross your path.

Law firm lawyers generally have greater access to a broader selection of pro bono opportunities than in-house lawyers. This is in large part due to the fact that many law firms, large ones in particular, have developed their own pro bono platforms, with an infrastructure built around providing their attorneys with a wide variety of choices. These days, many firms are opening these opportunities to clients and in-house counsel, not just their firm's lawyers. Trade associations such as the Association of Corporate Counsel partner with various law firms to provide their membership with access to a wide array of pro bono matters that up until recently were not easily accessible to in-house counsel.

For in-house lawyers, one challenge when looking for quality pro bono work is finding work within their specialty. We encourage lawyers to use pro bono work as a way to spread their wings beyond their comfort zone. They can look at pro bono work not just as a way to help others in need, but also as a way to learn something new and expand their skills in the process.

Breaking into the Non-Profit Board Arena

Board service is another way to give back. There are myriad ways to get onto boards. First, you need to think about where your interests and passions lie with respect to civic service. There are so many organizations to choose from, each with different missions, causes and ways in which they operate. Likewise, boards can significantly vary in terms of their level of activity, what they are seeking to accomplish and what they expect and demand of board members. You need to do your homework and understand what serving on a particular board entails.

You also need to understand that getting onto boards is often a process and may take time. You should figure out the best way to meet the people you need to be successful in your efforts. Sometimes, you must first be a volunteer at the organization, or you may need to reach out to existing board members and the executive director to learn more about how best to become involved. There may be people in your network who are past or present board members who can lend a hand. Other times, you may first need to develop a high enough profile within your community so that you are chosen to serve on the board, rather than the other way around. There are many possibilities, and the right one depends on you, your personality and the board on which you are interested in serving.

The board process may not be easy, especially when just starting out. Consider where your passions and commitments lie. If you are unsure, try volunteering with different organizations to learn what they are about, and which fit best with your interests. If your sights are set on a high-profile board when you are just starting out in your volunteer career, you may first need to get your feet wet with a smaller organization. Learn what it means to serve on a non-profit board and how board work fits within your life. Develop your reputation as a reliable and desirable board member. By demonstrating your interest and willingness to help others and being actively involved, in due time, you can move up to that high-profile board.

Finding The Right Balance

You need to be honest and realistic about your level of interest and commitment, both to yourself and to those recruiting you to join their board. You need to be very clear on where all of your priorities lie and where civic service fits into the grand scheme. This will drive your assessment as to how much time and energy you have and are willing to give to civic service. You also need to have a thorough understanding of a given non-profit's expectations and demands on your time and where it fits in with respect to everything else in your life. Knowing all of these things will help you to strike that delicate balance.

If joining a board is too big of a time commitment for you, volunteer for a committee, help organize a discrete program, or even do just one task for the organization. This way, you fulfill a genuine need, you feel a greater sense of connection to the organization and put in just the right amount of time.

Changing The Way People View Lawyers

It is unfortunate that people's perceptions of lawyers are sometimes quite negative, based on the few bad apples out there. Even though every profession has them, the public is often less forgiving of lawyers, possibly because of the special ethical duties and responsibilities lawyers have, and the gravity of the issues that attorneys typically handle. Christina explains, *"My first real exposure to these negative sentiments was when I was in engineering school. Many of my instructors and classmates believed that lawyers readily put a price on someone's life and that they show no remorse in doing so, particularly in the product liability context."*

What critics don't seem to appreciate is that lawyers are human beings just like everyone else, and that they care just as much, if not more so, about others than anyone else. People are often reminded of this when they see lawyers out in the community lending a hand on a pro bono basis to those who are less fortunate. Hopefully, as an increasing number of lawyers become involved in civic service, these unfair notions will be dispelled. When laypersons see lawyers giving their time, it enables them to see lawyers in another light - as fellow members of the community, lending their time and expertise to help others, at no charge.

Meeting Annual Pro Bono Goals

There can be a number of challenges when it comes to meeting annual pro bono goals, including finding the right subject matter for you. Some attorneys like to stick with their practice area, while others view pro bono as an opportunity to venture into a completely different specialty. The challenge then becomes finding someone to provide you with the necessary assistance to ensure that the matter is being handled properly. It can also be a struggle to find enough time to take on a pro bono matter. Depending on how active your matter becomes, it can be tough to balance the demands of pro bono with the needs of your everyday practice. From an organizational perspective, it is sometimes difficult to make sure that all lawyers are prioritizing pro bono and doing their part to ensure that the organization's overall pro bono goals are being met.

For in-house attorneys, one of the greatest challenges is finding pro bono opportunities that include malpractice insurance. Most in-house attorneys do not carry malpractice insurance, thus limiting their ability to handle matters for clients other than their employer. Another challenge may be licensing. In-house attorneys working under multi-jurisdictional practice rules in states other than their home state are typically limited by such rules to representing only their employer. Fortunately, that practice is changing, and some states, including Illinois, now allow licensed attorneys to also handle pro bono matters *(check applicable rules for details)*.

The Importance of Activities Outside of Work

It is important to have interests beyond your job responsibilities for a number of reasons. First, if these activities are chosen mindfully, they can enable you to have professional experiences that you may not otherwise get. Whether they are hobbies such as coin collecting, painting, mentoring or volunteering for a nonprofit, extracurricular activities provide many important benefits. You can develop certain skills, be exposed to new types of situations and gain knowledge that you otherwise would not acquire in your everyday job. Extracurricular activities are an opportunity to do something beneficial for and with others, and can provide the opportunity to meet new people, and to learn different perspectives and even new approaches to problem solving. You can also take what you learn and bring it to work to make your job performance even better.

It is important that you participate in activities that are meaningful to you, where you think you can contribute and where you believe you will be better for having the experience. Also, be sure that you meet as many people as possible so that you can make the most of the networking aspect of your activities. In addition, be sure to connect the dots before you say yes; think through whether the opportunity is likely to help you to accomplish your professional goals and to leverage your skills, contacts and interests such that one plus one equals three. And be sure to revisit all of these activities periodically to confirm that your participation still makes sense, and to step out of them if they no longer serve their purpose.

Be sure to ask enough questions to evaluate whether they are the right activities for you right now. Be clear on what you are trying to accomplish. Is this for professional growth and advancement? Or is it just for fun? You also should get clarity about what the time commitment is and whether there are requirements like hosting meetings or events, which may tip the balance. Finally, make sure that you are going to enjoy yourself. Anytime that you commit to something beyond your job, it is important to ensure that you find it worthwhile enough to outweigh the price of participation, both in dollars and in time spent away from your family, and any other trade-offs you may be making.

David explains, *"I remain passionate about the causes and the organizations I serve, however, 15 years is a long time on one board. It is important to recognize that burnout can start to set in, and also that there* comes a time to make room for others with new ideas. It is also important to recognize when you just need a break from doing organized extracurricular activities. After 30 years serving on boards, I needed a break so I took two years off. Once I had the opportunity to step back, I was then ready to join another nonprofit board. The break let me recharge. It also allowed me to consider what I can bring to a new board by building on my past experience."

Insights Into Our Unique Pro Bono Experiences

From Christina's perspective:

"I began my career at my first firm as a real estate lawyer with a focus on environmental law. Within a couple of months of joining the firm, a special project came in from Chicago City Hall. I was asked if I would be willing to join the City of Chicago Department of Buildings for several months to help it restructure the Chicago Building Code. The department was in the process of reviewing and revising the building code from cover to cover and wanted to include an outside lawyer as part of the process. My engineering background was a real asset for this project since there are many technical references within the code. The project went on for about half a year and I learned a great deal. It also helped me to understand how important relationships are, both personally and professionally. It was an amazing experience and I had a chance to meet Mayor Daley at the end of the project.

Now, when it comes to selecting pro bono work, I look at a few things, including the practice areas involved, how much time the matter is likely to take and the time frame within which it needs to be completed. I compare this against how much time I have and the type of project in which I am interested at that juncture. If I am likely to need the assistance of others, either within or outside of my practice area, I also consider the availability of those who am I am likely to tap before taking on the case.

The senior leadership at both of the law firms at which I have practiced have delivered the clear message that serving the underprivileged is the right thing to do and is essential. My first firm's leadership were key architects in creating its innovative international pro bono platform. Pro bono is required of every attorney at many large firms, including my current firm. We also actively partner with numerous clients on different pro bono activities, and it is an integral part of our business development efforts."

From David's perspective:

"Shortly after I started practicing law, I joined the board of a homeless shelter and services provider in Uptown Chicago. In addition to my board service, I provided legal advice to the organization over the years, including such things as responding to records subpoenas, various employment issues and drafting personnel policies and procedures. The bulk of my pro bono activities since going in-house have been participating in activities for improving the practice of law and the legal profession through volunteer service with the Association of Corporate Counsel. This includes not only through serving on the board of directors but also helping plan and present continuing education programs, helping run a summer internship program for law students and helping the ACC Chicago Chapter expand pro bono opportunities.

I am fortunate to work for a company which is owned by committed philanthropists. Our culture embraces the necessity and importance of giving back. I am also fortunate to have a boss who has supported all of my volunteer efforts over the years."

We all must remember those who are not as fortunate as we are and consider how we can help them. We must do our part to make a positive difference for those who are unable to fend for themselves. Consider whether there are pro bono cases you may want to take on that could help an individual or group in need of some type of assistance. Perhaps there are young students, or even rookie attorneys, who would benefit from meeting with you to discuss their potential career paths. Maybe there is a charity or organization that could greatly benefit from your time or money. Take time to visit a sick or elderly friend or family member, or to wrap and deliver presents for children whose families cannot afford to buy them. The possibilities are endless. Whatever you choose, however you decide to give back, know that your efforts and dedication matter.

We often believe that others are doing just as well, if not better, than we are. We tend to minimize the importance of the contributions we can make to others and to society. As lawyers, we are in a unique position to help people in ways that others simply cannot. Whether we are helping the wrongfully convicted, mentoring future lawyers, or providing financial assistance to the needy, know that anything we do for another person, either big or small, can have a profound impact and can change the course of lives. What better gift is there - to give or receive?

Resolutions and Goal Setting

As professionals, it is imperative that we not wait until the new year to pause and reflect on our successes and accomplishments, as well as our shortcomings. At any time we can commit to improving, whether that means being more productive, effective and successful at work, spending more time helping those in need or focusing on our physical and mental well-being.

All businesses are forced to change with turbulent times, in a very Darwinian sort of way. There is no doubt this evolution will continue at a rapid pace. For those who have been waiting for the flux and uncertainty to abate, it has become increasingly clear that what we are experiencing now is the new normal, and the only steady state we can expect is one of continual change. This should be no surprise, as many industries have been forced to recalibrate and reinvent themselves in a way that would have previously been unimaginable in the struggle to stay relevant, to be competitive and to survive. Although in many ways the professional services industry has historically been insulated from fluctuations in consumer demand and economic volatility, this is simply no longer the case. It is incumbent upon us to decide not only whether we will come to terms with and accept this paradigm shift, but whether we will embrace it and play an active role in shaping our collective future.

New Year's resolutions typically stay on our minds and in our consciousness for the first few weeks, maybe a month or two, into the new year. However, as with promises to save up for a new car or to lose those few extra pounds, our professional goals require focus, persistence and diligence and will require a permanent behavioral shift if we are going to successfully achieve them. We are invited to take a closer look at where we have been and where we are and figure out what we need to do to get where we want to go, both professionally and personally. In taking stock, we can reassess, recalibrate and formulate an action plan to maintain our focus in accomplishing our most important goals while following our passion and striving for inner balance.

The shifting paradigm invites us to take a look at the many different facets of our professional existence and to seek ways for us to better our performance and ourselves. Perhaps this is the time when you will strive to refine your client service skills and to become a more valuable member of your organization. Or you may decide that this will be your breakthrough year in monetizing your business development efforts. Perhaps you will set your sights on getting promoted or working toward that next leadership role within your company and taking your professional skills and performance to the next level.

Maybe you will focus on becoming a better mentor to the younger professionals in your organization. Or you may find ways to expand your skillset over the coming months to add to your areas of expertise. Perhaps doing more pro bono or volunteer work is your priority. Your goals may be more interpersonal in nature - for example, focusing on being a better listener, coming out of your shell and doing more networking, taking classes or enlisting the assistance of an executive coach to improve your professional and personal effectiveness. Whatever the case may be, we should prioritize and focus upon those goals which speak to us the most and be both aggressive and realistic about what we can reasonably accomplish. Being passionate about our careers, our lives and our professional and personal goals is contagious and excites those around us as well. Passion not only begets passion; passion also begets success.

Albert Einstein once said, *"Nothing happens until something moves."* This quote is such a profound commentary on myriad levels. Perhaps we should view Einstein's words as an invitation for us to think about how we currently view our careers and ourselves and to consider ways to change that thinking. Thoughts are very powerful and when we change the way we think about and approach something, we inevitably cause a similar shift in those around us. Together, we can profoundly change our professions and our world.

Calculated Risks Can Help in Reaching Our Goals

It is through examining our successes and shortcomings that we can more effectively formulate plans for the future and maximize our chances of accomplishing our short and long-term goals. Promises to ourselves, particularly when made as resolutions, are often unrealistic. Furthermore, we often underestimate the damage to our psyche and motivation resulting from having regularly unmet expectations of ourselves. Indeed, if we consistently fail to reach our goals, we often experience feelings of failure, inadequacy and low self-esteem which can then make it more difficult for us to effectively perform. Therefore, we owe it to ourselves to take a step back and make sure that we both consistently aim high while, at the same time, keep at least some of what we declare both realistic and achievable. Accomplishing even just one or two of the goals we set for ourselves creates the necessary traction for attacking other challenges and creating the "*flow*" in our lives where the real magic happens.

As we are setting our goals, we must be brutally honest and bold about the possibilities of what we can and should strive to achieve. Seizing greatness in our professional and personal lives is never easy and it is only by holding ourselves accountable and aggressively pushing to learn and grow as much as we can that we are truly successful. Rather than being distracted by what others are or are not doing, having the resolve to focus on our goals not only makes them more attainable but also frees up more time to take on additional interests and challenges. We should embrace each of the new opportunities we encounter along the way and see them as ways to learn about and improve ourselves.

While it is a challenge to be realistic in our goal setting and, at the same time, to push ourselves to the limit, it is in striking this balance that we are at our best and can then most effectively help others in their journeys to also be better professionals and people. We all know that life is full of successes and failures - those which life deals us on its own and those which we bring upon ourselves. However, we often forget this reality when we get down to developing that list of goals we wish to accomplish. We often end up playing in the minor leagues in the game of life, rather than setting our sights on the majors. If we all take a moment to reflect on what our dreams and aspirations were when we were children, we would realize that we all dreamt a little bigger when we were young. Some attribute this to the naiveté of youth, but in reality it may be because we have all become a bit disconnected from ourselves along the way. We owe it to ourselves to reconnect with who we really are, to think about what excites, motivates and inspires us and whether we have people and opportunities in our lives which will open up possibilities for joy. Achieving happiness is a sure sign that you are doing something right - and that success is likely around the corner.

Whether you ultimately succeed or fail in what you set out to do, there will undoubtedly be tremendous wisdom and knowledge gained in your journey. Indeed, many of the world's most successful leaders say that their greatest learning experiences have been in those moments when they have failed in what they have set out to do, rather than when they have succeeded. Knowing this to be true, we should all feel more confident in pushing our boundaries in making whatever resolutions or goals we choose, while at the same time maintaining a sense of realism in the process. Taking calculated risks is what life is all about. It enables us to push toward our most challenging and meaningful goals, while at the same time to follow our passions and maintain our zest for life.

Finding Inspiration in The Stories of Others

In our quest for self-improvement, we all look for inspiration in myriad ways. There is often profound wisdom in the personal accounts of others, particularly those who have accomplished great feats, notwithstanding tremendous personal struggle and tragedy.

US Supreme Court Justice Sonia Sotomayor's autobiography, *My Beloved World*, tells one such story. Her memoir is a candid, intimate account of her upbringing in a Bronx housing project as the daughter of Puerto Rican immigrants. There are many intriguing aspects to Sotomayor's experiences. She has shown remarkable courage and fortitude by not only surviving, but thriving under circumstances that would have destroyed many others. Being a Latina woman of modest means trying to make it in the male-dominated legal profession is only a small part of her story.

At a young age, she experienced a number of tragic events which had a significant impact on her life as well as on how she views the world and her place in it. Sotomayor was diagnosed with type 1 diabetes at age 7, at a time when many considered the disease to be a death sentence. By necessity, she became self-sufficient at an early age and learned how to give herself insulin injections. Her mother worked nights as a nurse to support the family and was often not at home. Her father was an alcoholic, which prevented him from being able to keep his hands steady enough to administer her injections. At age 9, Sotomayor's 42-year-old father succumbed to his addiction. His passing devastated her family and left an indelible imprint on her.

Notwithstanding these traumas, when she tells her life story, it is not as one who feels severely disadvantaged but, rather, as someone who believes she has lived a truly blessed life. She is a survivor, and notwithstanding all of the ill fortune and challenges she has endured, she has persevered and thrived through sheer force of will. She is passionate about the life she lives and her moral compass is focused on serving others. She is an inspiration to us all.

From Christina's perspective:

"I was deeply moved by Sotomayor's story in many ways, and there are a number of interesting parallels in our respective lives. I am the daughter of a Mexican immigrant who came to the United States in the 1950s with little more than the shirt on her back to follow the American dream. My mother barely spoke English and left her entire family behind in Mexico City in search of a better life. While she went on to have a family

whom she deeply loved and four children of whom she was extremely proud, she never realized her own professional dreams. Diabetes prematurely ended her life at the age of 50. I was a senior in high school at the time.

Sotomayor wrote that experiencing the death of a parent as a child makes you see the world very differently; I agree. Our ability to handle life's challenges are forever measured against the pain of that devastating loss and we feel at least some level of assurance going forward that we can weather practically any storm which may befall us. There is also the stark realization that everyone among us will experience ill fortune of some kind during our lifetimes and that it is up to us whether we will allow those experiences to lift us up or to beat us down. If we are willing, we can glean valuable lessons from these events. In doing so, we can all develop a more profound sense of empathy and deepen our understanding of each other."

These are all important lessons for us, both as professionals and as human beings. We are all a product of our experiences and we have an obligation to keep learning and growing and to continuously share our knowledge for the betterment of others. As we make sense of both the good and bad that happen around us, it is important to keep a balanced perspective and to focus on our primary mission as professionals, which is and always will be to serve others, notwithstanding the ebbs and flows of our own lives.

Sotomayor observed that possessing intellectual talent is a gift which serves a higher purpose and should be shared, particularly with those who are less fortunate. As you consider what is in store for you next and contemplate your goals and commitments, remember that your profession empowers you to make a meaningful difference for those whom you represent and serve. Sotomayor aptly states, *"There are no bystanders in life and our humanity makes all of us a part of something that is bigger and greater than ourselves."* It is in putting others first that we can find the greatest fulfillment and inspiration of all.

Carrying Forward Lessons Learned

As we reflect on our professional and personal lives, we have developed a list of lessons learned - or revisited - and hope that it will be a helpful roadmap on your journey, wherever it may lead.

- **Follow your passion.** It is essential that we commit at least part of each day to doing those things that we love. They will bring us joy and a sense of balance against those aspects of our lives we may not enjoy as much. We need to have hobbies and outside interests and should also strive for careers which bring satisfaction and fulfillment.

- **Live outside your comfort zone.** Success is acknowledging our strengths and fully leveraging them while also pushing ourselves beyond our existing boundaries into new terrain. Exactly how we should strike that balance is a personal decision and is driven by what we want to achieve as well as our hopes and aspirations.

- **Recognize and embrace new opportunities.** As we reflect on the major turning points in our lives, a few consistent themes emerge. First is the understanding that opportunity comes along more often when we are open to it. Second, the magnitude of change precipitated by certain opportunities is not always readily apparent at the time we are making the decision whether or not to embrace it. Indeed, opportunities often come disguised as impositions on our time or just more on our list of things to do. It is important to impart mindfulness to all that we do and the choices we make so that we can make sound decisions when opportunities do present themselves.

- **Focus on what matters.** We all have countless responsibilities and pressures in our lives, and it is easy to focus on those things which are vying most for our attention rather than on what matters most to us. Too often, we get sidetracked by projects, goals and agendas which in the grand scheme do not matter and are a waste of our time and energy. It is essential to separate the wheat from the chaff, to gain clarity about our priorities and to govern ourselves accordingly.

- **Maintain your focus.** Keeping our focus is essential in a 24/7 world full of nonstop stimuli, and it is easy for all of this noise to distract us in a way that makes us much less effective. In order to optimally perform, we must find a way to effectively juggle it all while at the same time maintaining our ability to focus on the task at hand and give it our full attention and consideration as if it is the most important thing in our lives at that moment.

- **Have a positive attitude.** Let's face it - no one likes to hang out with Debbie Downer, least of all our clients. We can always do a better job of keeping our negativity to a minimum, especially when we are with others. Positivity begets positivity, and if we encounter certain people or circumstances which are likely to elicit negative responses from us or vice versa, it is our responsibility to address these individuals and situations as constructively as possible.

- **Think outside the box.** This is particularly important since professionals are expected to provide thoughtful, creative solutions on a regular basis. We need to figure out how we can regularly free our minds and access that "zone" within ourselves which enables us to think strategically and innovatively. This is essential in unlocking our ability to perform at our full potential.

- **Dare to be different.** Painting outside the lines can be a good thing, especially when we live in a profession where our success greatly depends on our ability to meaningfully differentiate ourselves. We should think about how best to take our existing skillset and transform it into something unique and original that effectively speaks to those around us - whatever that may look like.

- **Be authentic.** How often do we encounter people who are inauthentic? Just like specious behavior is obvious to us, others can likewise sense when we are not being forthcoming about our true intentions or motivations. It is incumbent upon us all to lead by example and to bring our most authentic selves to our professional and personal lives.

- **Give back.** Giving can take countless forms and should be done in ways that speak to us and which make the most meaningful difference to others. Whether it is performing pro bono or volunteer work, mentoring young professionals we know or helping a student with a school application, we should look for ways to pay forward the wonderful gifts which have been bestowed upon us during the course of our lives.

Innovation, Technology and Artificial Intelligence: Growth in Motion

Innovation and technology are not just buzzwords. They are the beating heart of progress, the quiet (sometimes loud) revolution that transforms how we work, think, lead, connect and live. Whether we embrace or resist them, innovation and technology are always moving. The question becomes: Are we evolving with them?

Depending on the individual or organization, innovation can take many shapes. For some, it might mean offering services in a better, more efficient or more value-driven way. For others, it is about increasing the quality and quantity of products while minimizing effort, waste and cost. Sometimes, it is about solving one problem while simultaneously considering the ripple effects across the business and the community. Other times, innovation is doing what has never been done before, whether that is something others have imagined but could not implement, or something no one has even dared to dream of.

At its core, innovation is progress. It is also momentum and creativity in action. The word itself means introducing something new - an idea, a method, a mindset. Innovation pushes us beyond what is comfortable and challenges us to evolve, both individually and collectively. In many cases, it asks us to partner across traditional silos. Departments, disciplines and industries must collaborate to co-create better outcomes. In today's world, staying in your own lane is not enough. To remain relevant, effective and meaningful, we must think wider, reach further and build smarter.

The Case for Constant Evolution

Being innovative does not mean being flashy. It means being aware and vigilant. It represents growth, maturity, progress and relevance, especially in a 24/7 world that is moving and shifting incessantly. The ability to innovate separates the good from the exceptional, the stagnant from the thriving.

As professionals, leaders and people, we face increasingly complex problems. We cannot afford to keep using the same playbook for every new challenge. Our ability to adapt and approach problems from fresh, creative angles is not just helpful; it is *necessary*. It gives us an edge in business development, client service, and how we live and lead.

There is a Steve Jobs quote that still captures the soul of innovation many years later. When asked if he conducted market research for a project, Jobs responded that he didn't, because customers *"don't know what they want until you show it to them."* That is innovation at its most powerful - leading people to discover needs they do not yet realize they have.

When we innovate, we lead, shape, anticipate and problem solve. We are serving a higher purpose. And when we do it well, our clients, colleagues and communities come to see us not just as providers but as valued partners and visionaries.

Innovation is a Culture, Not Just a Concept

Implementing new ideas can be very challenging. It cannot be done in isolation, and it rarely works if we try to bulldoze our way through resistance. Culture eats strategy for breakfast, and innovation, by definition, threatens the status quo.

To innovate effectively, we need to understand the culture within which we are working. What does our organization value? How do our senior leaders make decisions? Who needs to be in the room, and who needs to hear the idea first to champion it? Moving individuals is one thing. Moving an organization takes strategy, patience and influence. It starts by building a coalition of leaders who believe in the vision and are willing to help support it - then change becomes possible. And often, one innovation begets another. Innovation is contagious, but so is fear. So, our focus needs to be on speaking to people in ways they can hear us (use your EQ), to meet them where they are and then, step by step, to move forward together.

Technology: A Double-Edged Tool

There is no question that technology has made our lives easier as professionals. Over the past few decades, it has transformed how we access clients, gather information and deliver services. Virtual private networks (VPNs), cloud-based desktops and video conferencing tools have allowed us to create functional offices from anywhere in the world. Smartphones put people and answers at our fingertips, and remote collaboration tools allow us to be global without ever leaving our homes. Email, social media and cloud-based systems have revolutionized how we communicate and store data. We are faster, more efficient and more connected than ever. And, with artificial intelligence (AI) evolving at breakneck speed, the speed of transformation is accelerating by the second.

Technology has also leveled our playing field. Sole practitioners and small businesses can now compete with corporate giants in ways which had previously been impossible. A stable Internet connection, a well-designed website, and a strong digital presence can open doors that never used to exist.

However, technology has also raised expectations, and not always in healthy ways. In the past, we had buffers built into communication. There was time to think, reflect and compose. Today, our inboxes are always bursting, our phones are always on, and people expect real-time responses. What once took days now takes minutes or less. And our stress levels skyrocket when the Internet goes out or a server crashes. For many professionals, the pace of technology has eroded the space we need for critical thinking, analysis and rest, and comes at a huge cost.

Contrary to popular belief, professional value is tied not to how fast we can respond but to *how well we think*. Technology should be a tool for innovation, not a treadmill we cannot get off of. If we are not careful, the very tools designed to empower us will start to control us. So we have to set boundaries, preserve time to be thoughtful and strategic, and protect our creativity for the asset it is.

Artificial Intelligence

Artificial intelligence, as a concept and tool, incorporates so many different things. The term has been part of our vernacular for quite a while, and it has quickly evolved from being this vague concept referring to the notion of computers doing tasks that have historically been done by people, to being everywhere all the time in every facet of our lives. There is very little in our society these days that is not touched by AI somehow, much like the Internet 25 years ago. It is transforming the world as we know it, and as with many things that we have seen during the course of history, it is incredibly powerful, and it is up to us to leverage its capabilities for the betterment of our lives, and to put sufficient guardrails in place to mitigate against its malevolent use.

David explains, *"As a lifelong Star Trek fan and having watched the first Terminator movie the night after my Contracts final first semester of law school, the fact that we seem to be on the precipice of the actual AI age is exciting and concerning at the same time."* What we will ultimately be able to use AI for both in life and in the practice of law, and how things will actually change over time, triggers some concern about the negative implications, especially for younger people just entering the practice of law, and for the job market generally.

From Christina's perspective:

"My use of AI in my practice, much like the technology itself, is evolving. Given where I am in my career, both being in private practice as

well as practicing for over 30 years, my use of AI looks very different day-to-day than for more junior lawyers. I have seen so much in my career, and rarely am I starting from scratch with my knowledge of an area or for developing frameworks within which to address those issues. I find AI tools particularly helpful when I am trying to update my understanding of a current issue and need some direction on where to turn to get that information quickly. My firm, like many others, has a set of law-related AI applications that are part of the suite of tools available to our workforce (and clients as appropriate), some of which you may not even think have AI running in the background."

From David's perspective:

"I have only recently begun actively experimenting with various AI platforms in my practice. I anticipate that I will increasingly and intentionally use AI tools in much the same way Tina described, particularly AI tools built specifically for lawyers, not simply the AI built into existing platforms like Microsoft Outlook to suggest email sentence completion or AI-generated internet search results for information about a TV show. Thus far, I have experimented using AI to help with initial drafts of some non-standard contract clauses, which has been surprisingly helpful, and to generate presentation outlines, with mixed results so far, though I have been pleasantly surprised to see similarities with outlines I wrote on my own the old-fashioned way using my own brain power. As AI tools become more robust and reliable, I envision using them to help with initial research into new or unfamiliar substantive areas of law and to help get past writer's block."

It is incumbent upon us to ensure that our use of AI aligns with various considerations, including compliance with our organization's AI policy and the policies of our clients. There are also important attorney-client privilege and confidentiality concerns, as well as weaknesses and gaps with the technology as it stands today, such as hallucinations. Lawyers also have a code of ethics to which we need to adhere, so ensuring the completeness and accuracy of the work product we generate while leveraging AI is of paramount importance. AI should always be used with good common sense as the backdrop, as with everything else, and used in moderation and with intentionality, particularly given where we are in its evolution.

A primary concern among many professionals is that using AI will cause a degradation and outright loss of people's ability to engage in critical thinking, analysis and writing. Another pitfall, given the promise of doing things faster, is that the demands on us to produce even more work and more quickly will steadily increase, which in turn will lead to a tremendous increase in the stress and burden of practicing law, along with an ever-diminishing ability to take a break. The idea might be that we work fewer hours because we can get things done faster, but the concern is that the opposite will in fact be true. Finally, there is the threat that some lawyers will neglect to read what AI produces for them and fail to recognize that what they are writing and citing in their briefs are in fact erroneous AI hallucinations.

Innovation Beyond Invention

Too often, when discussing innovation we focus solely on invention, such as the breakthroughs in science, medicine and technology that grab headlines and change history. But this unfairly narrow lens leaves many who are worthy among us out of the conversation. Innovation does not always come with a patent, nor does it have to be revolutionary to be powerful. Innovation can show up in how we solve problems, build relationships, approach leadership, and even in how we prioritize wellness in the workplace.

Innovation can be simple, subtle and quiet. It can be reimagining a client intake process, rethinking how we support team development, or finding more inclusive communication methods. The key is always the same: *Does this create progress?* That is where we start.

The Myth of the Lightning Bolt

In his book *Where Good Ideas Come From: The Natural History of Innovation*, Steven Johnson debunks the myth that innovation results from a sudden flash of brilliance. He reminds us that most breakthroughs are slow burns, ideas that evolve over time, built through collaboration, iteration and yes, failure.

Real innovation often comes not from the lab but from the lunchroom, not from the grind but from the gap, from taking a walk, reading something unexpected or letting your mind wander as you go about your day. The best ideas do not always come when we are *trying* to be brilliant. They often come when we create the space to connect the dots already floating around in our minds. We have to be willing to pause, play, daydream, experiment, ask questions and occasionally get it wrong. This requires humility, curiosity and trust - not just in ourselves, but in each other.

Collaboration is a Catalyst

If there is one truth about innovation, it is that it rarely happens in isolation. Even the most brilliant minds need connection. We need each other to challenge assumptions, offer perspectives and co-create solutions that are bigger and better than what any one of us could do alone. Too often though, we resist collaboration out of fear - fear of being wrong, looking foolish or losing control. But perfection is not the goal - growth and progress are. We should stop trying to be right all the time and start stepping out of our comfort zone because the magic happens in conversation and connection.

When we leverage our collective experiences, talents and ideas, we create something far more innovative than any individual could dream up alone.

Create the Conditions for Innovation

Innovation is not something you wait for - it is something you *invite*. And that invitation begins by making space for it. Just like technology companies build in time for creativity, such as Google's famous 20% rule, we too need to give ourselves permission to step away from the grind and into imagination. We must unplug, reflect and reconnect with our values and goals. We need to ask: *What are we doing? Why are we doing it? And is there a better way?*

When we slow down, we begin to notice what is possible. And often, the most meaningful innovation is not about doing something new. It is about seeing what was there all along in a new light. Ultimately, innovation is a mindset. Whether we are leveraging technology to better serve our clients, creating new systems that make our organizations more efficient, or simply finding a new way to approach an old problem, innovation is always about one thing: *growth*.

Innovation asks us to stretch, risk and reimagine. It invites us to lead with curiosity instead of certainty, collaborate instead of compete, and evolve instead of entrench. In doing so, it helps us become not only better professionals but better humans.

Skills of a Great Professional

This chapter is devoted to just some of the countless skills of a great lawyer. While this is by no means a comprehensive list, we explore some of what, in our experience, are the most important attributes of the exceptional lawyers and mentors with whom we have had the pleasure of working and learning from.

Being Indispensable

Being indispensable means that you are essential and mission-critical. You are crucial to have as part of the team and the organization. You are necessary to accomplish a particular goal, in making it through the day to day, and an invaluable part of the decision-making team such that your input is not only desired but essential before a final decision is made.

In the context of practicing law, this term is often used to refer to a particular skillset or combination of qualities that you bring to the table that makes you someone people feel they cannot live without. This is essentially a client-focused concept. For in-house attorneys, the goal is to become indispensable to both the business as well as other attorneys in the legal department. The same concept holds true within law firms, as you not only want to be indispensable to your clients but also to other lawyers at your firm.

As with many aspects of our legal careers, becoming indispensable starts with getting to know as much as possible about your client's business; this goes for both in-house and outside counsel. In addition to gaining a deep understanding of what your client's business is and how it works, you should also get to know the businesspeople - the C-suite and beyond; learn what they do, what is important to them, and how they do their jobs. Get to know them as people; learn to speak their language. The easiest way to accomplish this is to ask them questions and carefully listen to their answers. Demonstrate by your conduct that you are a dependable and essential part of the team, as invested in the outcome as they are.

If you are indispensable to your clients, you are better able to provide meaningful advice, help your client manage risk and avoid unnecessary and costly missteps. You are also more likely to be valued and retained. Being indispensable also enhances career enjoyment and fulfillment.

As organizations evolve over time, so do the workforces within them. Employees have different experiences over the years which drive their capabilities, relationships, responsibilities and tenure. These factors all impact performance of the individuals and the teams they comprise. Hopefully, people are given the opportunity to fulfill a role that is not duplicated by anyone else on the team and for which they are uniquely qualified and needed. As one matures in their career, they can then become indispensable in any number of different ways, which helps ensure that they continue a long and meaningful professional trajectory over time.

What makes you indispensable today does not necessarily make you so tomorrow. We have seen instances where people spend a lot of effort trying to convince others that they are indispensable without doing the hard work of actually becoming so - and then a situation arises where it becomes evident that life can and will go on without that person. We have also seen the flip side - where people are not given the credit that they deserve until they leave an organization, and then it becomes clear that they have been undervalued. The moral of the story is to remain keenly aware of what you and those around you bring to the table, both individually as well as collectively, and manage and lead your team from that place.

Another step to becoming indispensable - bring solutions, not just problems, and train your clients and business colleagues that they need to immediately call you, even if they are not sure whether it is a legal question. Then make yourself available, listen to them and provide a solution. By demonstrating your versatility in your willingness to work on a broad variety of matters, and being practical with your advice to better minimize risk and maximize the chances of a successful outcome, you can show your colleagues, clients and management that you are an indispensable member of the team.

Being Nimble

As we balance our goals, work and family routines, we should be mindful that change remains the constant undercurrent in our lives. Nothing is static and we are constantly on the move, which presents myriad opportunities and challenges. While all of this uncertainty can make us uncomfortable and apprehensive, it is in our best interest to both adapt and leverage this dynamic reality to our advantage. Being nimble is a critical part of this equation.

Merriam-Webster's Dictionary defines "nimble" as, *"quick and light in motion,"* and *"marked by quick, alert, clever conception, comprehension, or resourcefulness."* While these two concepts are interrelated, they are actually quite different and call upon distinct skillsets. One relates to action and movement and feels reactive, while the other describes one's thought process, is strategic and seems more proactive. Both concepts provide us with useful guidance for navigating the ups and downs of today's business environment and help ensure that we are responding appropriately.

Being nimble enables us to adapt and react to the rapidly changing circumstances which impact our clients' businesses on a daily basis. We are able to see how their needs may be evolving and respond to events in their environment, and consider how we may need to quickly alter our tack in order to effectively address the circumstances they are currently facing. As nimble practitioners, we are not discouraged by the possibility that our past recipes for success no longer work and that we may need to self-correct. Instead, we are flexible, resilient and able to respond quickly to the current reality. We seek to understand the genesis of change and where it is likely to lead in an effort to enhance predictability and so that we can better position our clients and ourselves for what is next.

There are many ways in which our practices can benefit when we are nimble. We are better able to create business opportunities in the face of uncertainty. We can quickly and accurately predict changes that may be afoot which are likely to impact our clients' organizations, and we are able to adjust our approach accordingly. Sometimes these changes are swift and can range anywhere from significant events in the life cycle of their businesses such as acquisitions, divestitures or compliance issues to a forced change of counsel due to an unexpected conflict. Whatever the situation, being nimble enables us to be there for our clients in their hour of need in a more meaningful way and to continuously demonstrate our value as their trusted advisor. We are not intimidated by the prospect of expanding our existing client relationships beyond just our area of expertise. Rather, we embrace the opportunity to learn more about all of their legal business needs and to take a more holistic approach in our work with them.

These types of efforts are both welcomed by clients and can pay great dividends in the long run. Being nimble also enables us to be more strategic in the ways in which we develop relationships with prospective clients. This is particularly true during challenging times such as a recession, when there is significant disruption in the market and when the old rules no longer apply. At such times, it often becomes more difficult to find ways to differentiate ourselves. We must all demonstrate both sophisticated substantive talents and equally important soft skills, which are often tied to high performance and critical areas such as client service and relationship management.

Being nimble is another arrow in our emotional intelligence quiver and enables us to effectively strike this delicate balance from one potential client to the next. No two businesses have the same legal needs and by being nimble, we are able to quickly discern how best to present our capabilities in a way that resonates with our audience and to adapt to swiftly changing circumstances during our initial meetings and communications. We are able to think outside the box, spot issues and provide logic and insight as to how best to address them. Being thoughtfully and strategically quick on our feet provides another way we can meaningfully stand apart from our competition.

Just as our clients are barraged with new opportunities and challenges on a daily basis, so are we. It is very important for us to nimbly position our organizations and ourselves with the same amount of savvy and foresight as we bring to our clients. This means that we must be vigilant about the business of our business and must never lose sight of those qualities which will ensure our short and long-term success. We need to regularly evaluate what effectively distinguishes us in a particular geographic market, within certain practice areas and in a given business sector. We should be continuously aware of who our competition currently is and who it is likely to be tomorrow as well as those characteristics which successfully differentiate us all from one another. By doing so, we can more accurately predict how certain issues are likely to evolve over time and more effectively leverage these changes into opportunities for our organizations and ourselves.

Being Multidimensional

Being multidimensional means that you bring qualities, talents and attributes to the fore, which enable you to tackle numerous issues and myriad matters with aplomb. You are able to analyze situations from different points of view which are appropriate for the circumstances. You are able to communicate, strategize and execute wearing a variety of hats. You are resilient, flexible and nimble. It includes drawing upon a combination of legal knowledge, business knowledge, emotional intelligence, and an understanding and awareness of other areas such as culture and current events. The ability to do this is facilitated by having multiple and varied interests in life. You might look at it as the diversity within you.

This is invaluable from both client service and leadership perspectives. It enables you to be more out of the box and non-linear in your thought process and gives you the ability to be more effective in your problem solving. It provides different lenses through which to observe the world and the ability to empathize with clients and colleagues so that you can avoid having tunnel vision. Being multidimensional enables you to work with many different types of clients with ease and to work with the same client across many different situations. It is not so much about being the subject matter expert across distinct legal areas as it is having a heightened awareness and sensitivity that enables you to meaningfully contribute in various situations to address the relevant issues quickly and effectively, either on your own or with the assistance of others you choose to bring in. We live in a world where lawyers need to differentiate themselves, and this is one way to do just that.

The broader your interests and curiosity, and the more you are open to new experiences, the better equipped you will be to approach client matters from different angles and to advise your client not just on black letter law but within a context that makes a practical difference for their needs. Being multidimensional makes it easier to form relationships with different types of people, which not only leads to being a better and more successful lawyer, but also leads to more fulfillment in life generally. For example, most attorneys will agree that the excitement of contract drafting tends to wane after drafting hundreds of them. Boredom can lead to mistakes. So, it is important to find ways to maintain your interest and thereby sharpen your focus on what is truly important in the contract. This is considered taking "the 50,000-foot view" of a situation to understand what the contract means in the larger context of a company's business, the customer's business, even the economy as a whole. This will help you to better understand the broader benefits and pitfalls beyond the document in front of you, which leads to better lawyering and greater career satisfaction.

It is a delicate balance between being multidimensional, and a specialist who requires frequent evaluation and recalibration. The right balance is highly dependent on where you are now and what you want to achieve in your career. If your goal is to have a thriving prolific practice, you must be a great lawyer, stay on top of new developments, continuously look for ways to perfect your craft, make yourself known and to differentiate yourself in the market. If your objective is to be in leadership, there are skills you need to develop and hone that go far beyond just being a respected practitioner and typically involve a level of executive coaching and management training that will help you develop your skills. Striking the right balance requires you to be strategic and to prioritize what is of greatest importance to you. It is a highly personalized exercise.

Finding a balance between being multidimensional and a generalist involves handling many different substantive legal matters that arise across multiple business sectors, involving myriad factual scenarios. Being multidimensional helps you to understand and give advice that better meets the overall goals and needs of your clients. It also helps you to work well with many different people at all levels within your organization and with your customers and vendors. David explains, *"I think it is also why I thrive on the variety and breadth of my practice and the rapidity with which new matters come to me every day, enabling me to constantly be learning and growing as an attorney and as a person."*

Being Unique

When you are unique, you stand apart from the rest. You have a skillset, attitude and approach that make you different. When people look at the totality of who you are - your personality, your talents, your clients, your actions and your contributions to the profession - they automatically know it is you, even if your name is not mentioned. There is a lot of self-awareness that comes with the territory, as well as the ability to authentically embrace who you are as both a professional and an individual. You need to be able to own what makes you unique and you should not be afraid to follow the beat of your own drum.

There are certain guitar players who you know just by hearing them play a song, such as Eric Clapton or Jerry Garcia, or just by hearing their voices, such as Bruce Springsteen or Bob Dylan. Being a unique lawyer is similar in many ways. They are known for certain specialties or skills that instantly set them apart. Some lawyers are unique because they have a practice that few others share, or they have developed a reputation for being distinguished among other practitioners in their specialty. Some lawyers are notable for doing things in a particular, ideally positive, way. Maybe you are known for your cross examination or conflict resolution skills. Uniqueness may lie in superior writing talent or advocacy skills. You may have a knack for relationship building or management skills. These are the things that differentiate, that set you apart when others think about you, or that make others think of you when they are in need of a particular skillset.

Oftentimes it is a delicate balance of knowing when to stand out and when to blend into the group. You want to stand out for positive, selfless reasons, such as doing a great job on a client project or in a pro bono case. It should not be premeditated on your part, and you should not be standing out for the sake of standing out. When tooting your own horn is appropriate, it should be done thoughtfully, carefully and respectfully. For example, when doing business development, you should focus on those skills that make you valuable and unique and play up your strengths. This will help potential clients to distinguish you from your competition much more easily. You should always be respectful and avoid gratuitously criticizing your competition, since that is unseemly and unprofessional.

Sometimes it is better to blend in when, for example, you are working on getting a project done and out the door. That is when being collaborative and a team player are most important. Everyone on the team has an invaluable contribution to make. While there are certain team members who will inevitably stand out more than others, such as the team leader, they should not be forceful or overly assertive about it. It is important that everyone works well together and is collaborative rather than engaging in power struggles.

Blend in by showing that you fit with the organization's culture, mission and platform, but again, only so far as to ensure you do not stick out like a sore thumb and make others turn the other way. You want to blend in to the point that others consider you a team player. At the same time, you want to make sure you maintain your individuality and demonstrate that you are an impact player and making a positive difference.

Young lawyers need to focus on standing out for the right reasons. These include doing great work, working incredibly hard and showing maturity and wisdom. There is simply no substitute for having that fire in the belly and a willingness to go through brick walls for clients. They should demonstrate that they are deep thinkers, highly intellectual and emotionally intelligent, and that they have a strong business savvy.

Young lawyers also need to demonstrate drive, focus and integrity. Show that you are not afraid of the difficult work or long hours. Demonstrate perseverance, poise and determination when working on difficult assignments under demanding circumstances. It is also important not to complain about the long hours and hard work. That will get you noticed, but not in a positive way. Be a leader and speak up with solutions when there are problems.

Being Creative

Another way to stand out is to be creative, someone who can think outside the box and who is able to see issues from a variety of angles and perspectives. Creativity is realizing that the best solutions for clients are often a hybrid of good lawyering, good business and good common sense. Creative lawyers ask clients what the ultimate objective is in a given situation and ask them what they are trying to achieve. They realize that there are often a myriad of ways clients can achieve their goal, and those options usually pose different levels of legal and business risks, costs and short and long-term impacts to the business. Sometimes the optimal solution entails a minimal amount of substantive lawyering but nevertheless presents a great opportunity for creative lawyers to put on their business hat and to serve as a trusted business advisor. A creative lawyer is also someone who can effectively put themselves in the shoes of their clients and other interested parties and understand where they are coming from and how their viewpoints factor into reaching the best solutions. They can meaningfully brainstorm without constraint and, once all the ideas are out on the table, they can then go back and figure out which solutions are optimal.

Creativity encompasses more than just good writing and coming up with novel solutions, although they are important components of being creative. It also means discerning ways to effectively communicate with clients, opponents and colleagues. This can be done in different ways, such as by conducting training sessions on various topics and discussing why they are important to the business and the consequences of various choices. Other aspects of creative lawyering include a willingness to try new things and challenging assumptions - just because it has never been done before does not mean it is wrong. Also, collaborate and seek input from colleagues - teamwork can lead to very creative solutions.

When it comes to a lawyer's individual style, there are a number of key factors. The most obvious is our outward appearance, including how we dress and present ourselves. Our demeanor is another critical component, and it transcends how we look and drives how we come across to others. Our demeanor refers to those qualities and characteristics which others notice about us and what they would say when describing us. It is a critically important aspect of our style, and there should be alignment between how we think we come across and how others actually view us. Disconnects in this regard can often be tricky to navigate and can have significant consequences. Indeed, our demeanor is inextricably linked to our overall effectiveness with other aspects of our style, including how we perform and in our approach to clients and business development efforts. Our style often makes the difference in our ability to land that new client or to resolve a difficult case.

We can all learn a lot from watching others and seeing what works and what does not. But we must then take stock of those qualities and characteristics which resonate the most, tweak them and carry them forward. Developing a unique and creative style that works should give us a level of comfort, confidence and self-assurance which then optimizes our interactions with others and enables them to feel like they know us and what we are all about. Predictability is key, and is all about balance and nuance.

We need to be authentic but also act within acceptable bounds based on our environments and audiences. While we all want to meaningfully distinguish ourselves from the crowd, we want to stand out for the right reasons rather than the wrong ones.

Navigating Office Politics

People talk about office politics because it is instrumental in determining whether you succeed long-term in an organization. Unfortunately, it is often a black box. Many people do not fully understand how office politics work and often feel helpless, particularly when things do not go their way. Office politics is an inextricable part of one's experience in an organization and is critically important to understand, but is so often misinterpreted or ignored, in the hope that it will disappear. However, as long as there are people involved, there will be politics.

Workplaces are an amalgam of people - those who want to get ahead, those who want to get along, those with tremendous intellect and drive, and those who merely want to skate. Office politics exists in all workplaces, whether there are thousands of employees or only one. It is human nature that most want to get ahead in the workplace, especially in organizations filled with large numbers of bright, driven people. Office politics is really a derivative of the social contract.

People often mistakenly give up the control they have on their professional path by chalking up whatever happens to them to office politics, rather than owning the situation and taking responsibility for what they can meaningfully change. There will always be certain things we cannot fix in our lives - and our working environment is no exception. However, we should not throw the baby out with the bathwater by completely relinquishing the control we do have.

Another misperception is that you can rely solely on what people say and do in trying to figure out the politics in your workplace. There are other dimensions - one's attitude, motivations and personal agenda - that are essential to recognize and figure out with those around you. You need to take a step back and understand what people say and do in the context of how they approach work so that you can better predict what they are going to do in any given situation, as well as where alliances lie and how certain situations are likely to play out. The predictability factor is critical in determining how you should best react, if at all, to any given situation. Office politics is not all about manipulation and backstabbing, nor do you have to play dirty to get ahead.

There are many lessons to keep in mind when it comes to managing how you engage in, or steer clear of, office politics. First, be realistic about whether the politics as they exist in your workplace is something you can successfully navigate and whether you can be happy and fulfilled at work. Second, you need to acknowledge the games people play. Things are not always what they appear to be; be cautious about what you believe, particularly when the information that comes to you is hearsay. Understand there is usually a spin put on everything, either intentionally or unintentionally.

This segues into another lesson learned - be careful what you say and do. You can be the straightest shooter there is, but if the people around you want to create drama, they may take something you say or do which is very straightforward and innocuous and spin and manipulate it to serve their purposes. That is why it is really important to have at least one person at work whom you can completely trust, and who completely trusts you, so that you can share information and help each other navigate the politics. It is always good to have someone who can help you think through what is happening and how to handle certain people and situations, and help ensure things do not come back to bite you.

David explains, *"During law school, my father, also a lawyer, taught me what I consider the essence of office politics: A little bit of brown-nosing never hurt anyone; too much will kill you."*

Mastering Delegation

There are only 24 hours in a day. Delegation enables you to get more done in less time when tasks are broken down into various pieces and done in parallel. Having people you can delegate to creates leverage, which is essential to staffing matters in an economical way, especially in an era where we must do more with less. It also helps ensure team members are focused. For those tasks that have already been mastered by certain co-workers, you should look for ways to involve other team members who can benefit from receiving cross-training on those tasks. Delegation is critical because no one person can do or know it all. It is important for efficiency, economy, training and creativity.

Delegation is a dynamic, not a static, concept. Over time, the best delegation evolves as people's skillsets grow. It takes into account how people are learning, developing and mastering various skills. It is important to strike a delicate balance of delegating the right amount and the right types of tasks to the right people. This means mastering the art of breaking projects into smaller pieces, knowing the resources available to you and their respective skills, and project managing each to ensure timely, effective completion. You must also consider what pieces of a project you will do yourself, whether you are growing through the process and giving yourself an opportunity to shine as well. Making the decision not to delegate at all, or to delegate less than you should, particularly in a professional services environment, is not what clients want. It is taking the easy way out and it is self-limiting behavior. Delegating too much can have its own problems, including taking significant risks with the quality of the product and losing control of a project. Through effective delegation, you learn what colleagues can do well and where they excel.

We often think delegating is too difficult and that it is easier to do things ourselves. Successful delegation of certain work is essential to our own successful performance. The key is being able to delegate to the right people who will get the job done well.

If you are in a situation where you are unable to delegate as much as you would like you should consider your options in terms of getting the work done that you have. This involves taking inventory of projects, what the deadlines are, how long they will take to complete, what you can reasonably expect your schedule to look like, what your other daily obligations will be and what juggling will look like. If you are in-house, you may be able to send some projects to outside counsel or, if you are part of a legal department, see if others can lend a hand with at least some of the work. If you are in a law firm, think of how to get both immediate and longer-term help, as the one-person-band model does not generally work in the long run.

Delegation is not just pushing work down to a direct report or someone more junior than you. It is a form of teamwork. Delegation often means relying on your non-lawyer business colleagues to help with work, which helps support the business as a whole.

Be Focused

Being focused is one of the key ingredients to performing at an optimal level. It makes you more effective since you are able to concentrate on thinking through issues and projects much more clearly and comprehensively. Focus also enables you to get into the flow more often and more seamlessly, which gives you the ability to have more frequent "aha" moments and to push the boundaries of your creativity. It also makes you more efficient at the various tasks you perform so that you are able to handle a greater volume of work over a shorter period of time. All of these factors contribute to enhancing your performance, which will ultimately help you to differentiate yourself in the marketplace.

Focus also enables you to drown out the noise of outside distractions, enabling you to maintain your train of thought and, quite simply, to get your work done. Focus enhances delivery of good client service. More than just focusing on paperwork, the concept includes focusing on the person you are with. Whether that person is your boss or your client, they will have a much better experience and appreciation for you and for the interaction as a result of you giving them your full attention.

When you are distracted by things going on around you rather than concentrating on what is in front of you, it can be tough to focus. It is easy to become scattered, which often happens when you are not completely clear on what is truly important to you and then developing your list of priorities based on those things. If you are spread too thin, or overtired and overly stressed, it can have a paralyzing effect. It is also tough when your work environment and habits are not conducive to developing and maintaining your focus. It is like having a finely tuned instrument or a well-developed muscle - it requires a significant commitment and determination to concentrate on the present moment, to the exclusion of everything else.

There are so many distractions during the workday. Days are filled with the telephone ringing, clients walking into your office, a constant barrage of emails - all of which are raising new questions and issues across a broad spectrum of substantive areas and most assuredly disrupting your intended schedule or agenda for the day. This can be quite jarring to your ability to focus. However, this explains why focus is so important, especially the ability to focus quickly on each new issue while pivoting from one person to another, one matter to another, one substantive area to another.

There is a certain mindfulness that is necessary in order to maintain your focus, particularly over a sustained period of time. The trick is to figure out how to get yourself to that place. Christina explains, *"I learned how to meditate a number of years ago and have found that it helps me to quiet my mind and get more in touch with my intuitive side. This helps to create a sense of inner calm and peace within so that I can stay more focused on what I am doing and remove the clutter of my mind so that I can perform to my full potential."*

It is also critical to develop a work style and environment that enables you to concentrate on what is in front of you. Whether it is turning off your phone and email for a while and closing your door, or taking a walk to clear your mind before jumping into a project, you need to develop ways that help you minimize distractions. These methods will vary from person to person. David explains, *"One technique I use is working to music; I actually find its absence distracting. I meditate every morning before leaving for work and I recommend taking breaks once in a while to clear your head, even if you just take a few seconds to close your eyes, take a couple of deep breaths and center yourself."* You might also try starting your day by clearing several smaller tasks off your to-do list so they do not nag you while you are trying to focus on a longer or more difficult task. If you need to focus for a long period of time on a single project such as writing a brief, try a change of scenery - working from a coffee shop, library, a conference room instead of your office or a different room in your house.

Humility

We often hear about humility, whether we are discussing human interactions in the context of business or world relations. It is a rather elusive virtue often in short supply, yet it is essential in our ability to take meaningful steps forward in many areas of our lives. Merriam-Webster's Dictionary defines "humility" as *"freedom from pride or arrogance."* Although it seems simple enough, it is exceedingly rare to see true humility in action. As one of the core emotional intelligence attributes, it is a key component in both transforming our organizations and in bettering ourselves as professionals.

So, what does humility look like? It means we put others before ourselves and strive to get beyond the surface in our communications in an effort to connect with other people in a more thoughtful, meaningful way. It is appreciating the importance of hearing other's points of view, thereby creating an environment conducive to sharing viewpoints, one where everyone feels like they are truly being heard. Listening plays an essential part in the success of this dynamic, and true collaboration is a byproduct of the process. It is creating a sense of "we," not just "me" and "you."

Humility is also understanding that we do not know everything there is to know, and that others are able to contribute just as much, if not more, than we can to a particular situation. It also means that we are not always prioritizing ourselves, our wants and desires. Instead, our attention is consistently focused on the needs, wisdom and contributions of others and what is best for the collective whole.

With humility, we recognize that we are not perfect, and we make a concerted effort to conduct ourselves in alignment with that knowledge. It means that we have come to terms with that aspect of ourselves, and it is a willingness to acknowledge our shortcomings to others. There are many lessons to be gleaned through the process of making mistakes, and it is through this imperfection that we experience a sense of vulnerability. By being able to convey this sentiment to others, we have an ability to relate to them and to understand different sides to issues and various points of view.

This, in turn, makes us more effective in our interpersonal communications in the long run, since we project a sense of accessibility, approachability and camaraderie that is essential in successful relationship building and decision-making. We cannot overestimate the importance of humility in our client relationships, and it is a critical element in effective client service. Our clients look to us as wise and knowledgeable counselors in our respective practice areas and expect us to effortlessly demonstrate that they chose wisely when retaining us. Whether they express it or not, they also expect us to strike that extremely delicate balance between consistently demonstrating our quiet confidence and displaying a healthy dose of humility.

While clients do not set out to hire wimpy lawyers, they most certainly do not want to be subjected to needless arrogance. It is our responsibility to be the very best practitioners we can be, and to believe in ourselves and in our ability to do our jobs effectively. At the same time, we must carefully modulate our behavior and attitude appropriately and make sure that our priorities lie first and foremost with our clients, rather than ourselves. When interacting with them, we should always ask ourselves if we are listening to what they are saying and reacting accordingly, rather than merely telling them what we want them to hear and what makes us feel good about our own expertise. True humility means a lot less talking and a lot more listening.

Humility is also an extremely important component of effective leadership. The best leaders intuitively understand there are myriad ways to achieve success, and it is often a product of synthesizing the thoughts and ideas of those whom they lead, rather than any independent epiphany the leader may experience. Projecting humility is a critical part of engendering the type of dialogue and sharing of ideas necessary to arrive at a desired result. Having that likeability factor and being able to instill confidence in others through empathy inspires others to act and are the hallmarks of a truly effective leader.

Ultimately, humility is a true selfless act, not a weakness by any means. In fact, it takes a great amount of strength and resolve to consistently demonstrate humility, both professionally and personally. And just as it is abundantly clear when we are seeing humility in action, it is likewise patently obvious when it is absent. As CS Lewis so wisely stated, *"Humility is not thinking less of yourself, but it's thinking about yourself less."*

Likeability

The analysis seems simple enough - if people like you, you will be happy and successful. But if it were that easy, then why isn't everyone doing it? The likeability factor - sometimes referred to as the LQ, for likeability quotient - remains an elusive concept. There is often an inherent tension and fundamental misunderstanding between the reality and fiction of what makes us likeable, what we should do to be more likeable and whether it is even important. And while we may believe we have an intuitive sense of all of these things, we are often shallow and misguided in our notions.

It is only in the past few years that we have even begun a meaningful conversation about likeability and its effect on our happiness and success. The simple fact is that we cannot have a robust workforce that will effectively perform over the short- and long-term if mutual admiration and collegiality do not exist in our workplace. We cannot effectively create client service teams if our colleagues who are essential to those relationships do not like us and want to help. Given that our professional world now consists of a waning demand for many types of legal services, clients have a multitude of great lawyers to choose from, and they simply will not work with us if they do not like and respect.

So, what does it mean to be likeable? It means we can readily relate to others, and vice versa. We do so by establishing common ground in relationships quickly and easily. We are thoughtful, engaging and focus on those with whom we are interacting in the moment, rather than allowing ourselves to become distracted and multitasking our way through a situation. We effectively empathize and see clearly the lens through which others view the world. We understand others' points of view, demonstrate that we truly hear what people are saying and act in accordance with that understanding. We meaningfully convey that we sense both the good and the bad that others feel and tailor our approach appropriately to the situation at hand and offer our assistance.

We are also authentic and genuine in our communications and create alignment between what we say and what we do. We bring a certain level of excitement to our professional and personal circles because of the passion we bring to all that we do, and that sentiment is contagious. Those around us feel like they have a strong sense of who we are and what we stand for and enjoy being with us. Indeed, trustworthiness, credibility and predictability are all critical ingredients of being likeable.

There are a few underlying themes here. Our ability to connect with others is an essential element of the likeability factor. As part of that, we need to gain an understanding of what motivates and inspires other people. What are they hoping to achieve, and how can we help them get there? How can we adapt our approach so that what we say and do is most impactful for them? Connecting with others is inherently a two-way street, and we need to remember that it is not all about us. In fact, being likeable is very little about convincing others how great we are and is much more about our ability to understand the people around us.

In determining what makes others tick and uncovering the common ground we all share, we should make a concerted effort to consider different points of view and listen carefully to what others have to say. We also need to be thoughtful in how we respond. Our most powerful communications are strategic and well-timed. We should also be keenly aware of our strengths and weaknesses and brutally honest with ourselves about what we do well and what we need to work on. We must take a close look at ourselves and ensure we are attuned to what others really think of us. The impression we make is a combination of many factors, including our intellect, personality, appearance and demeanor. It is important to have a positive attitude and understand that it is a powerful force that more readily precipitates the desired results upon which our clients and organizations thrive.

We also need to regularly take stock of the nature and quality of our interactions with others. We should be attuned to how we feel during these encounters, both mentally and psychologically. We must listen to our body, and whether we feel settled and balanced, or uneasy. We can pick up on the energy of others and how they are feeling by paying close attention to both verbal and nonverbal social cues. Sometimes we need to step outside ourselves and actively seek this type of feedback from those around us whom we respect and trust. This may include working with executive coaches and other similar professionals.

In considering what it means to be likeable, it is also important to know what it does not mean. Likeability is not about winning a popularity contest, nor does it mean that we are pushovers. In our quest to be likeable, we must be authentic and comfortable in our own skin. We cannot be everything to everybody, and there will be times when others may not like us, no matter how hard we try. And that is okay. While we should be sincere in our efforts to understand others and in treating them as we would want to be treated, we also should not take ourselves too seriously. None of us is perfect, and just making a good-hearted effort to connect with others will often go a long way.

Gravitas

Likeability is an important component of the overall package we offer clients, and its close cousin is gravitas. It is often used interchangeably with words such as charisma and executive presence. The Oxford Dictionary defines gravitas as *"the quality of being serious and dignified in manner, often commanding respect and trust."* and, according to the Urban Dictionary, it is *"strength of character, self-esteem, confidence."* Wikipedia mentions that gravitas is one of the Roman virtues, along with Pietas, Dignitas and Virtus and that it *"conveys a certain substance or depth of personality."*

Notwithstanding the fact that it is defined in any number of ways, gravitas still remains a bit of a conundrum. Historically, the term has mainly been used in the political realm, but as it has become an increasingly mainstream concept, it is often applied in other contexts, including in the media and business world.

As with other things which defy a clear-cut explanation, you know it when you see it. People with gravitas exude success, have an air of authority and leadership and command respect. They are effective communicators, they garner credibility and convey a wisdom often attributable to both age and experience. They have a level of confidence which is readily perceived by others, yet without projecting a sense of arrogance. Those with gravitas are authentic and align what they say with how they think and what they do, which makes their communications with others much more powerful and impactful. They project selflessness as their way of being, rather than selfishness.

There are a number of different components to gravitas. First, there is a certain level of substantive knowledge, intellectual horsepower and focus which is critical in establishing gravitas. We are able to successfully leverage our strengths but also recognize the limits of what we know and understand what we do not know, which allows us to seek the assistance of others as needed. This serves the greater good and is key in maintaining our credibility. Our appearance and demeanor, which include how we look, dress and present ourselves in both formal and informal settings, are also important. There is a level of assertiveness and self-assuredness which goes hand in hand with gravitas, and these are inextricably linked with our posture, body language and level of engagement when interacting with others.

Maintaining eye contact, having a firm handshake, delivering effective presentations and projecting our voice when speaking are just a few of the many examples of how we exhibit gravitas. Being a great communicator is also an essential ingredient. This means that we are able to take our knowledge and insight and successfully and passionately convey them to others in an inspiring way. We wholeheartedly believe in what we say and say what we believe. We are persuasive and project confidence and composure in our oral and written communications. When we have a healthy dose of emotional intelligence, we have the tools to take these communications to an even higher level, since we are finely attuned to ourselves and others. We are keenly aware of our audience in any given situation and understand the various points of view.

We hear both what is said and unsaid and are able to read the room for clues and suggestions on how to make adjustments to our approach in real time. Maintaining a high-level of engagement in a situation is an important element of gravitas. Developing and maintaining gravitas takes a lot of hard work. There is an age-old debate about whether it is something we are born with. As with most things in life, there are those who seem to effortlessly demonstrate gravitas, whereas others have a more difficult time with it. Regardless of which camp you are in, everyone can take steps in developing and harnessing gravitas. Working with professionals such as executive coaches and soliciting honest, frank feedback from friends and colleagues about our personal effectiveness and our strengths and weaknesses can be effective tools in our development. We also need to recognize that gravitas is not about bowling others over with how great we are. Rather, it is in the process of meaningfully connecting and making a positive difference, and in being kind and generous in the service of others, that our true essence, our gravitas, shines through. Whether we are born with it or are cultivating it from scratch, we must always look for ways to improve ourselves and our skills.

Gravitas is not just for politicians, newscasters and the C-suite anymore. Indeed, it has become increasingly important for all professionals, and lawyers in particular. Having gravitas helps to inspire the trust, confidence and peace of mind of clients. Given the continued evolution of the legal and business landscapes, clients are always seeking meaningful differentiators among their various service providers. Gravitas is often part of that "secret sauce" in the recipe for effectiveness and success.

Listening

We hear it all the time - there are few talents in a lawyer's arsenal more important than being a good listener. Listening is an essential component of effective communication, both as attorneys and as human beings. As children, we are taught early on that if we listen to our parents and teachers, we will be successful. As adults, we often lose the wisdom of this powerful lesson. Although simple in concept, effective listening nevertheless remains an elusive skill and is often difficult to do well.

There is usually a confluence of factors which leads to communication challenges. First, we all see the world through our own set of experiences and predispositions, each of which acts as a filter in our interactions with others. Thus, when we listen to what someone is saying to us, there can be a huge gulf between what that person is actually saying and what we are hearing. Our ability to effectively listen is also shaped by our overall feelings about the message being delivered as well as the person delivering it, either positive or negative.

We also live in a world of perpetual distraction, often making meaningful communication difficult. We are incessantly bombarded with a wide array of stimuli - the calls, emails, texts and meeting requests we receive all day every day. In our zeal to quickly juggle these demands through the fine art of multitasking, this sensory overload makes it easy for us to lose the essence of any given exchange. It takes special effort on our part to ensure that we do not pay short shrift to others, particularly clients, in this process.

Most people prefer to talk rather than listen, especially lawyers. There is a common misperception that those who talk the most are inevitably the smartest in the room or should garner the most respect, which is simply not the case. Rather than always trying to figure out what to say next, we should prioritize focusing on what others are saying to us in the moment and processing that information. Listening does not display weakness; rather, it shows respect for another person and demonstrates a true interest in understanding their point of view.

Sometimes communication gaps occur when the person we are speaking with does not say what they really mean. This often happens when there is an underlying fear of how others will react to the message or when there is a larger agenda at work. The discerning listener can nevertheless capture the real message, being sensitized to what is not being said and other nonverbal clues.

With all these communication issues, how can we ensure that we listen effectively, especially with our clients?

First, focus on the speaker. Provide your full attention and do not multitask. If necessary, turn off your phone, email and other distractions, particularly in a face-to-face meeting. Think generally about the other person, what you know about them, how they view the world and where they are coming from with respect to the issue being discussed. Think about how their position as well as their prior experiences may color and shape what they are saying and how they say it. Also consider how you would feel if you were that person and what you would be saying if you were in their shoes.

Then pay close attention to what is being said. Do not just listen to the words; also listen for the tone of voice and cadence, as well as for pauses, when those pauses occur and other similar cues. Watch for the presence or absence of nonverbal body language, such as facial expressions and eye contact and for posture and gestures. These clues can tell you a lot about the general mood of the speaker and how they are feeling. Do they seem happy, sad, angry, impatient, frightened, overburdened, skeptical, aloof or otherwise? Is their sentiment something they are merely feeling in the moment or is it more of a general state?

As you are listening, also consider why the person is speaking with *you* about this topic. Sometimes the answer is immediately obvious, but not always. You need to determine what is being requested of you, if anything. Are you being asked to take some sort of action or to provide advice, or are they merely bending your ear or venting? Understand that the person may not come right out and ask for your assistance. If the purpose of the conversation is not immediately evident, ask yourself whether there are bigger issues at play and consider whether there are any other dots you need to connect. This includes figuring out who else is involved and what is at stake in this situation for all of the relevant players.

As you are engaged in discussion, be sure to react appropriately. You should not only provide cues that you are both understanding and processing what is being said, but also follow up with ideas and questions as appropriate. As the conversation winds down, consider what is most appropriate under the circumstances to ensure that the other person feels heard and understood. This can be anything from developing an action plan to offering an expression of support or just agreeing to pick up the conversation again soon.

Sound simple? It can be, if you are focused and understand just how essential effective listening is to being the consummate professional. Just remember that as lawyers, we cannot deliver what a client wants, needs, and expects if we do not hear what they are asking for.

Passion

Finding passion in one's career can be an elusive quest; the law is no exception. Indeed, many lawyers express long-term dissatisfaction with their jobs and seek their true passion elsewhere. In fact, they will often stop practicing law altogether and take the plunge to pursue other interests on a full-time basis. Why the endemic unhappiness? We have all heard countless times that the law is a "jealous mistress," all-consuming and an endless source of stress.

This myopic view is typically born of the adage that the grass is always greener on the other side and fails to recognize that every other profession has also become much more demanding and stressful. There is little, if any, indication that those demands will ever abate. So what can we do? Channel your focus and energy on making the most of your career here and now and change that which is within your control, accept what we cannot change and have the wisdom to know the difference.

Being a positive force in our profession is born of passion. Passion is a critical part of any successful and fulfilling path. It is what motivates and excites you. Passion fills you with energy and a positive attitude and enables you to work tirelessly. It is at the heart of finding satisfaction in what you do, both personally and professionally. Satisfaction breeds happiness and happiness breeds personal and professional success. It is difficult to find one without the others. Passion also makes you more powerful and effective with clients and potential clients. They are well-aware that passion translates into dedication and delivering results on their matters. It shines through in all that you do and separates you from your competitors. It enables you to focus, reason and problem-solve in a much more meaningful way. Clients both want and expect their lawyers to go through brick walls for them, and passion enables you to preserve and push through to the finish line, despite the toughest of challenges. Passion converts inaction to action, and results rely on action. Passion also provides a more impactful framework within which to both lead and mentor others. When you are passionate about what you do, others will want to be around you and follow your lead. There is a heightened level of engagement and excitement that you bring to the table. Your team will be more receptive to your suggestions, ideas and advice and will perform at a higher level.

When team members are focused on the same goals, it enables them to be much more successful in driving the desired results, both individually and collectively. In addition, when you are passionate about what you do, your mentoring is more likely to resonate with mentees. When you share your experiences with them, your passion is palpable, contagious and attractive, and they will want all of the excitement and motivation that they see in you. You will inspire them to take a closer look at themselves to evaluate their current circumstances and to determine where their own true passions lie. Everyone has a passion - it is just a matter of finding it.

Whether you are helping others find their passions or seeking your own, it can be a challenging endeavor. Passions rarely fall into one's lap, and finding them often involves hard work. In many ways, it is not all that different from dating and is a journey of hits and misses before you find what you are looking for. It is both an internal and external process, and while you must look outside yourself to determine what interests and motivates you, it is important to remember that passion is a state of mind and, in large part, comes from within.

As with finding a mate, if you are jaded and pessimistic, you will have a more difficult time, but if you are patient, positive and have an open mind, you are much more likely to be successful. There may be myriad reasons why you are unhappy today which have little, if anything, to do with lacking passion. Following your passion does not mean perpetual bliss, and just because a career or circumstance is imperfect does not mean that passion is lacking.

Finding your passion is an evolutionary process that can and should unfold over many years. As people change and grow, so do their passions. By frequently considering what inspires and motivates you, you can continue to mold and shape your personal and professional life. Tweaks, rather than monumental changes, will often be enough. Ultimately, you may be one of those individuals who finds that the law is not your true passion and you may instead decide that finding success and fulfillment means that you must follow a different path.

Effective Practice Management

Whether within a law firm or a law department, practice management means ensuring that the client always comes first. It means successfully getting clients, doing a stellar job on the work and proliferating those relationships, and making sure the right talent is in place to service the work and to grow the business and keep it moving forward. It also includes developing strong relationships with all business colleagues, appropriate business stakeholders, and other key players.

There are many key ingredients to successfully managing a practice. Substantive lawyering is what drives the engine - and if you and your team are not great lawyers first and foremost, it makes it very difficult to successfully build, grow and manage a practice. For that reason, having a strong talent management program is key - particularly for associates - so that they get substantive, real-time feedback and can learn how to be better lawyers. A critical part of the teaching needs to be about client service, which goes way beyond just getting the right legal answer. It includes knowing how to properly frame the advice and understanding client's expectations on deliverables and becoming their trusted advisor. The financial aspects of managing a practice are also crucial. This includes ensuring there is alignment between how clients define value and what a particular matter will end up costing them. As with every other business, bills need to be timely paid to keep the lights on, and metrics such as utilization, realization and profitability are regularly examined.

Practice management involves a lot of moving pieces, and you need to make sure they all fit together in a way that makes sense and creates a pathway for success. It takes a village to sustain and propel a practice forward, and everyone should be respected for the part they play. Furthermore, practices are not static - they are fluid and dynamic - which means that people's roles will morph and change over time, particularly as they gain new and different experiences. It is important to take a step back and evaluate the situation holistically on a regular basis so as to make periodic adjustments in response to these changes. And just as those around you will evolve over time, so will you - so you need to look in the mirror often and think about your own growth process and where it is leading you.

Being Proactive

Being proactive means being at least several steps ahead, and seeing around the corner, for your clients and yourself. It is understanding the current state of affairs and how they came to be and where the situation is likely to head, given the balls that are currently in motion. It is acting in response to that knowledge, and not just allowing things to happen through the ordinary course. Being proactive is often discussed in the context of preventing bad things from happening, but can also be viewed as optimizing the ultimate outcome of any given situation.

Being proactive manifests itself differently in different practices and organizations, but generally, as a lawyer means being out in front of matters, taking the lead, and not necessarily waiting for your client to ask the question. Take the initiative rather than waiting to react. Some things require reactivity, such as lawsuits. However, you can use those situations to be proactive, such as advising a client how to avoid similar situations in the future, or perhaps suggesting certain additional terms for contracts or revising processes and procedures.

From Christina's perspective:

"As a young attorney, I channeled my efforts toward doing the very best job on every assignment. I looked at projects on an individual basis. As I have gotten more seasoned, I think more holistically about clients, rather than on a matter-by-matter basis. I try to understand the currents driving my clients' businesses and their legal needs. I seek to be much more multidimensional in my thinking, and in developing my skillset and an understanding of the business of law and how global political and economic issues shape certain events and have ripple effects on all organizations. Thinking about the world and my clients in this way enables me to be a better predictor of what is coming down the pike and enables me to think, plan and react accordingly."

There are many ways that lawyers can improve their proactivity, beginning with thinking more thoroughly about more issues more often. This will enable you to better understand how events and circumstances are much more predictable and within your control than meets the eye. It is important to be a student of human nature, and understanding people's motivations and agendas is a significant part of that, since those things will often drive certain actions and failures to act which, in turn, lead to various outcomes. Critical thought and analysis coupled with a healthy dose of psychology will serve you well in your quest to be more proactive.

Sometimes, being proactive is as easy as cultivating relationships with your clients. Get to know them as human beings as well as businesspeople. In turn, they will feel comfortable and compelled to seek your advice and counsel. Knowing your clients and their needs opens the doors to learning what is important to them and to the business, as well as to providing advice and suggestions ahead of the curve, rather than waiting to react.

Professionalism

The concept of professionalism has expanded significantly, and the term is used to refer to many more facets of a lawyer's performance than in the past. It used to focus on ethics and ensuring that you do not run afoul of the rules of professional conduct. Now, it more broadly encompasses your actions, behavior and attitude toward those with whom you interact - everyone from opposing counsel to clients, colleagues and others you encounter. Professionalism also gets to the heart of what motivates you as an attorney, what your focus is and even your personal brand. It makes you stop and ask yourself what others who know you would say about you. Law is a profession whose duties and responsibilities are a 24/7 proposition and pervade one's entire life. You cannot compartmentalize it.

While the perception of it has changed, professionalism itself has not. It remains the hallmark of the best lawyers - those who conduct themselves honorably, ethically and honestly, treating others with civility, striving at all times to achieve justice, fairness and the best possible results within the bounds of the law. The attitude toward professionalism and the practice of law generally has changed, with a continuing decline in civility, such as litigation gone awry with the focus on procedural gamesmanship rather than resolving conflicts on the merits, in the best interest of the clients, as quickly as possible. Lawyers are officers of the court, whether one practices in court or not, and what we do, and how we conduct ourselves, reflects on the institution of justice. When we conduct ourselves professionally, it reflects positively and fosters trust in the law and respect for lawyers.

Lawyers are competitive by nature. In large part, this quality helps you overcome whatever obstacles you encounter in your quest to succeed. Being competitive can enhance one's performance, which in turn drives better results for clients. However, this is never an excuse for lacking professionalism. Your reputation and integrity are at stake when you do things that demonstrate a lack of professionalism. Furthermore, lawyers in particular have to worry about tarnishing their reputation. We are in a service business, and if you compromise your reputation, you jeopardize your ability to generate business and to otherwise succeed in your practice. We also have to abide by a code of ethics, and if we run afoul of those rules, our licenses are at stake. Balancing these interests can be done effectively by following the golden rule. If you are thinking about pursuing an approach that you would find inappropriate if done to you, it is a strong signal that you should not do it.

A lawyer's competitiveness should be informed by professionalism. Everyone wants to win, but winning at all costs may well be antiethical to professionalism, especially if you are motivated by personal factors. David explains, *"Years ago, I represented a client in an acrimonious commercial litigation matter. Leaving the courthouse following a long day in a mediation where I first met opposing counsel, I said to him, I think we could be friends if we met under different circumstances. Fast forward several years, we are now good friends and I have used him as outside counsel in other cases. We competed intensely in the courtroom and became friends outside of it.* " This is how you balance competitiveness and professionalism. There is nothing wrong with being competitive, but do so with honor.

To improve your professionalism, you need to stop and think about what you are doing, or not doing, before you do it, and think about the potential consequences a few steps down the road. If necessary, seek the advice of people whom you hold in high regard. You should also continue to develop yourself as a professional and as an individual and engage in activities that will help you learn and grow. Finally, you should do what you can to avoid being put into situations where your professionalism either can or will be compromised.

Most people become lawyers because they want to help others, so you have to remember that we are a service profession. Be of service to others first, and be genuine about it. Always treat others with respect and dignity. Allow others whom you hold in high regard to be a role model and then pay it forward. For example, when opposing counsel clearly has chosen the high road over other options, find a way to tell them that you recognize their choice and appreciate it. That acknowledgment can go a long way as that instance of professionalism gets paid forward again.

Project Management

Effective project management is key because clients demand it. We see it with the trend in our industry towards alternative fee arrangements and other mechanisms which are making billable hours more obsolete. Just as certain industries such as manufacturing have successfully used principles of project management for years, the legal profession and other service industries such as medicine, accounting and consulting have evolved in such a way that their projects are likewise being broken down into their constituent parts and analyzed closely to drive greater overall efficiencies. There are various elements that go into effectively managing a legal project, including bringing in the right mix of talent that is both efficient as well as cost-effective. This analysis can become quite complex and requires skill in predicting how long the project will take, by when certain tasks need to be completed and by whom. It is also necessary to have a good sense as to where the project may go off the rails along the way and to have contingency plans lined up.

In this era of increasing pressure to perform at the highest quality for the lowest possible cost, project management is essential to success and organizational longevity. It is important to enable lawyers to complete their work efficiently, expeditiously and thoroughly. David explains, *"As an in-house lawyer, I cannot plan or manage projects in a legal vacuum. I must work closely with my business teams to discern their needs and goals and to understand the nature, scope, extent, resources and timing of any given matter. All of this is critical to successfully supporting my business colleagues and my company."*

The discussion about project management has evolved from being a somewhat avant-garde concept in the context of a legal practice to an essential skill in the toolbox of every lawyer who is trying to effectively manage client matters. Christina explains, *"Years ago, I studied project management as part of my Industrial Engineering Degree and, at the time, many people thought that service businesses such as law were mutually exclusive from this type of discipline. Now, nothing could be further from the truth."* Effective project management is crucial to help ensure that a firm is providing its services in the most streamlined, cost-effective way while also making sure it is maintaining the necessary margins to make the work worthwhile for the firm to perform. The principles of project management are simple: planning, processes, people and power. In addition to doing the requisite planning to be able to map the necessary processes and the people who will help execute it, you also need to know where the authority/power lies for decision-making.

The methodology of project management tends to be the same regardless of the task at hand. It begins with carefully defining what you are trying to accomplish, both substantively as well as from a timing standpoint, and then reverse engineering the project from there. There are both hard and soft deadlines built in along the way, with contingency plans in case the necessary resources get delayed or are unavailable, or if the results the client was hoping for do not come to fruition. This is a process that many attorneys struggle with, so we recommend that you make a concerted effort to master the principles and techniques of project management in order to put them to effective use in your practice.

Sound Decision-Making

Decisions. We make them all the time - at work and at home. Sometimes they are easy, and sometimes they are hard. Where to go to dinner, where to go to school, where to live, where to work. Our lives are filled with decisions both big and small, and we are forever living the consequences of the choices we make. A fundamental paradox of decision-making is that we often do not fully appreciate that we are making a weighty decision in the moment we are making it. Indeed, we often spend more time on the rather irrelevant decisions than we do on the important ones. That is because of the inherently uncertain, fluctuating nature of the world. When it comes to matters of great consequence, we often need to react very quickly, and we typically do not have all the time and information we need to fully vet the issue before making a judgment call.

The book *The Greatest Business Decisions of All Time* by Verne Harnish and the editors of *Fortune* magazine is a provocative commentary on leadership and decision-making through the examination of 18 different business decisions that fundamentally changed the course of various organizations. Some of them even precipitated a profound shift in a particular industry and in the world. There are a few important lessons about making business decisions that emerge from those stories.

First, we must have a supportive team around us whose skills and talents are complementary and readily adaptable. Second, it is critical to acknowledge that we may not know the right answer in advance, and we may need to be in the moment and make a game-time decision. We must also understand that, as leaders, we are not always able to gather all the data we need to make a decision, and we often have to rely on others to do the necessary due diligence.

Attorneys are acutely aware of the fundamental dichotomy between legal and business decisions. It has traditionally been our responsibility to advise clients on the legal risks presented by various options, and it is generally the client's role to make the ultimate decision as to how to proceed, given the context of their business. Since time immemorial, we have been very reluctant to go beyond the four corners of legal analysis and have historically taken the view that we are either ill-equipped to make business decisions or that it simply is not our place to make them.

We must recognize that while on the surface this division of labor may exist, there is much more to this dynamic than meets the eye. There is always a business context within which legal decisions are made, and in order for us to do what we do and to do it well, we must understand and implement the fundamentals of sound decision-making, from both the legal and business perspectives. We must also demonstrate to our clients that we are able to seamlessly straddle both worlds and can see the issues at hand from all of the relevant angles. Whether we realize it or not, we as lawyers are constantly making business decisions. Whether we are deciding to take on a certain matter, go to a networking reception or send out a work document now or later, these are all business decisions in some shape or form. But we typically do not recognize these choices for what they are and underestimate their importance.

In those moments when we are fortunate enough to recognize that we are making a business decision of great significance, we must separate truth from fiction rather than seeing things the way we hope or wish them to be. We have to be clear about our identity and what our goals and aspirations are in the context of our values. We need to be realistic about seeing the issues and challenges presented by the outside world and what is changing around us. We then need to reconcile who we are with the realities of our environment and determine what we are best positioned to do and what that will look like. It is through striking this delicate balance among numerous competing factors that we are ultimately able to make the best business decisions for ourselves and our organizations, both in the short- and long-term. Our clients need to know that we have strong decision-making skills and a keen intuitive sense and are able to perform, regardless of whether we have weeks or seconds to analyze a problem. Through effectively wearing both hats, we can then become a trusted advisor and successfully navigate the business of law.

Each of us makes a wide array of decisions every day, some of which are small and some significant. While we try to put thought into every decision we make, it is the small decisions each day that will take a back seat to the bigger ones, particularly if time and resources are limited. Christina explains, *"There are several steps I take, particularly while making the more significant decisions. First, I start by acknowledging when I am about to make a decision of consequence - there is something about doing that which shifts my focus and thought process in a meaningful way. I then gather as many facts as possible so that I can fully understand the context and different angles to the issue at hand. I also try to connect with those who have a vested interest in the outcome and who may have had to make the same or similar decision in the past."* It is important to see as many different facets to an issue as possible, and to hear from those upon whom you will rely to both support and help implement the decision.

As lawyers, we reason by analogy and make decisions based on that. Some decisions are easy to make quickly, while some require more in-depth analysis and consideration. David explains, *"Exactly how I make decisions depends on the type of issue involved, and for the most part I draw upon the facts, my experience, judgment and knowledge of law and business. I gather as many facts as possible and try to consider all possible issues and angles. I will likely talk to others who have a stake in the outcome. Then I synthesize everything and make a decision. I do not use a formal decision tree and analytical tool, much to the chagrin of my engineer wife and brothers-in-law. Nevertheless, there is a logical process in my thinking."*

Arriving at the right decision requires striking a delicate balance among several factors - fact gathering, consensus building and going with your gut. Even if everything seems to generally check out, if you feel uneasy about a particular decision, your intuition may be telling you that further vetting or consideration of the issue is in order. There are some decisions that benefit from the input of a trusted advisor, someone with whom you can discuss tough decisions and not take it personally if they tell you something you may not like hearing.

The common thread in many decisions is letting go. This can be a very difficult thing to do, even though it is often what is best. Having faith that things generally work out the way they are supposed to can be helpful in navigating these challenging inflection points.

Taking Risks

Taking risks is a fundamental part of life. It pushes us to meaningfully learn, grow and adapt and enables society to progress. Risk poses an interesting paradox over time. In our youth, many of us are willing to take risks of all shapes and sizes, sometimes at potentially significant physical, emotional or financial expense. Some call it foolish, others call it having little to lose. Over time, we often experience a marked shift in our relationship with risk and how it fits into our lives. Most people become more risk averse as they get older. This is often attributed to the wisdom one gains over the years and life experiences that come with time. Many believe that the more successful they become, the more they have to lose and, as a result, they are more mindful of the potential consequences of taking risks. Fear of failure sets in and often quells one's desire to step outside the norm and try something different, whatever it may be.

Fear and risk-taking are often closely intertwined. While fear has its place and can effectively protect us from danger, we must also recognize when it lacks foundation and do our best to properly modulate it. For some, taking risks is just not part of their personality and they are risk averse by nature. Many of us lawyers fall into this category. Those characteristics which make us uniquely qualified to advise clients regarding risk mitigation inevitably push us to perform the same analysis for ourselves and often leads us to steer clear of risk. We cannot help it - it is simply part of our DNA.

We must constantly strive to effectively balance numerous competing factors in our lives. Risk-taking should be no exception. We need to effectively discern those risks which may be a stretch but are nevertheless worth taking - the calculated risks - and those which are not, and we must govern our actions accordingly.

We should be willing to make mistakes along the way or, to at least, expect that circumstances may not turn out exactly as we wanted. We need to understand that encountering the unexpected does not mean that the venture was not worth it. Ultimately, being successful does not mean we have never failed. Rather, it means having a life rich in texture as a result of myriad experiences which make us grow and enable us to enjoy its many facets without regret.

We also have to welcome the serendipity that manifests itself in our lives and the benefits - and risks - that are often presented as a result. Risk is usually wrapped into those unique opportunities which arise and which we are compelled to pursue. Life is full of surprises and has potential for great rewards. We just need to see and recognize this, be willing to stretch and step outside our comfort zone and not allow our fear to control the situation, or us. We must also understand that on the other side of risk and fear lies the potential for great reward.

From Christina's perspective:

"Risk has played an important role in my life. Many years ago, I was a college student studying manufacturing. I began pursuing my Master's Degree in Safety Engineering and had worked for two summers at Motorola and received an offer for full-time employment upon graduation. My mother had recently died and finances were a significant struggle for my family. I was paying for my own education and was looking forward to graduating from school and beginning my career as an engineer. The plan seemed perfect and much of its perfection was in its predictability - until I was accepted into law school. My head was saying I should defer starting law school for a year; work as an engineer and save money. But my heart and my intuition were telling me something different - that I should delay starting my engineering career, jump into the deep end and start law school.

There were a number of significant risks associated with this option - finances, job prospects and the big unknown of a legal career, as I was the first in my family to go to law school. Ultimately, after much consideration, I decided to go to law school straight out of college. While there were moments I felt truly overwhelmed and feared that I had made the wrong decision, or the right one at the wrong time, I now look back more than 30 years later and know that it was the right thing to do and do not regret my decision for a moment."

Being a Trusted Advisor

Being a trusted advisor means that you are a client's go-to person to discuss a wide array of issues, both within and outside of your practice area. You are a confidante, so that when concerns arise and decisions are being made, you are one of the first people who your client wants to consult. You are an invaluable partner and resource with a high level of credibility and trustworthiness. In addition to having the requisite book smarts and education, you also have a very practical wisdom that enables you to understand the overall context of an issue or problem from various angles. You are also caring and empathetic, and while you revel in your client's successes, you are also often up at night worrying about the matters which matter to them.

Trusted advisors have built a level of trust and confidence with clients so that they not only seek your advice but rely on you as their go-to consultant/advisor/sounding-board before they move forward on a particular project or decision. To be a trusted advisor means you are known for having particularly strong judgment, credibility and trustworthiness, and others come to you for advice and consultation as a result.

Everyone wants a trusted advisor, especially clients who are often called upon to make complex, multifaceted judgment calls at lightning speed. They appreciate being able to call upon lawyers with industry knowledge whom they trust implicitly and who can draw from a breadth of relevant personal and professional experience to assist in their decision-making process. Having this type of dynamic enables a more effective flow of information and allows for a greater level of candor and understanding which helps ensure optimal decision-making. Being able to develop and maintain a trusted advisor relationship is also significant in differentiating yourself from other lawyers in the marketplace.

Being a trusted advisor is one of the hallmarks of being a lawyer and is essential to one's success in the profession. Those with the reputation of being a trusted advisor enjoy the greatest career success - this could mean money, titles, personal satisfaction or fulfillment. Generally speaking, lawyers like to help people and to make a difference for others. Being a trusted advisor is emblematic of success in achieving those goals.

Becoming a trusted advisor requires skill, commitment and time. You have to be good at developing relationships with clients, and there is a certain level of rapport that is essential before a client will let you in. You must have an innate understanding of the client as a professional and as a person and what makes them tick. You have to have their best interest at heart and make their problems your own. No matter how challenging a situation may be, clients always have to find a solution which optimizes a number of competing interests - rarely will the answer *"it cannot be done"* work, so your suggestion needs to take this reality into account. It is also critically important to remember that all clients are people with strengths, weaknesses, fears, responsibilities and opinions of their own and that they are trying to do their best in any given situation. By being a strong sounding-board, you can create long-lasting relationships built on mutual admiration and respect.

There are many different paths, elements and traits to becoming a trusted advisor. You must possess strong judgment, ethics and morals. Gaining a depth of knowledge is critical, not simply about the relevant law but also about your client's business and the issues you are working on with them. It is also essential to know your client as a person. This is yet another example of where emotional intelligence comes into play and is so important. To become one's trusted advisor, you have to develop a close bond. This does not require friendship - that helps but is not required - but it does require developing a relationship built on mutual trust and respect. Impeccable honesty, judgment, credibility, reliability and authenticity are traits that enable one to become a trusted advisor for others.

Leaving a Legacy

Leaving a legacy starts with working on causes bigger than yourself. Making your mark means much more than just making a name for yourself, although that can be part of it. It is about the lasting impact you leave on your profession, your clients, your community, and the world. It is about showing up in ways that matter, not just once, but again and again, so that your influence lives beyond you.

To make your mark is to leave an indelible impression. It is not just about your reputation or your brand, but about the contribution you make over time. Most people, particularly those who are called to serve, lead and advocate, strive to leave the world better than they found it. That ongoing work - and the choices you make in how you show up, support others and give back - is your legacy.

We acknowledge that not all imprints are positive. Some people leave behind a trail of destruction, ego or neglect. But we deeply believe that professionals, especially those with a heart for service, can and should strive to make a positive, meaningful difference. To be remembered, not just for what you did, but for how you made people feel. That is what we call outstanding professionalism, and is the kind of legacy to which we aspire.

A Legacy Is Built Through Action

As professionals, we are in a uniquely powerful position. We possess valuable skills, insight and access. What we choose to do with those gifts matters.

Each of us can use our expertise to uplift others, support our organizations and improve our communities. We can start by identifying what we care deeply about and taking meaningful action in those areas.

Whether that is mentoring a new professional, doing pro bono work, writing and speaking on topics that educate and inspire, or leading efforts that promote equity and inclusion, one's legacy is forged through service.

The people whose lives you touch will then go on to help others, creating a ripple effect far beyond what you will ever see. That is the power of paying it forward, and is how your legacy lives on, magnified and multiplied.

There is no one-size-fits-all approach to making your mark, and there are countless ways to do so. Some are big and public, while others are quiet and deeply personal. Simply being an example of excellence, day in and day out, inspires others to strive for greatness and that, too, is a legacy.

Why Does Legacy Matter?

Legacy matters because it connects us across the past, present and future. When we think about what it means to leave a legacy, we consider honoring those who came before us, supporting those who walk alongside us, and paving the way for those who will follow. It is a way of paying it forward while remembering those who left their indelible impressions on us.

Legacy is also how we share our hard-earned wisdom, the lessons we have learned and the values we hope others will carry on. It is how we make our knowledge useful to future generations and help ease their path. And it is also a way to leave an imprint of ourselves, and to show others that we mattered. Ideally, one's legacy is a testament to what one has accomplished, how one showed up and who one has impacted. It is about aligning one's values with one's actions. On a very practical level, it also makes good business sense. When you become known as someone who does excellent work and lifts others along the way, your reputation precedes you. People want to work with someone they admire, respect and trust. Generosity, service and integrity attract opportunity.

How to Build a Professional Legacy

You do not need power, fame or fortune to build a legacy. What you do need is intentionality. Start by considering your organization's systems, frameworks and processes. How can you create something that not only makes things better and more efficient today, but can also stand the test of time? What can you design or improve that helps your business grow and evolve, even when you are no longer leading it?

Also think about your relationships. How are you contributing to others? Are you mentoring younger colleagues? Are you helping to diversify your profession by opening doors for those who have been historically excluded? Are you actively working to make your workplace more inclusive, equitable and ethical?

Leadership matters, and so does follow-through. Sometimes, your greatest impact may come from outside your day job, such as serving on nonprofit boards, volunteering in your community, speaking up for those without a voice, or simply modeling courage and kindness in everyday interactions.

Legacy does not always look like a grand gesture. Often, it is the accumulation of small, thoughtful actions over a lifetime.

Christina's Legacy: A Family Rooted in Perseverance and Purpose

"I am fortunate to have learned at a young age the importance of dreaming big and believing the sky is the limit, thanks to the unwavering support of my family, especially my parents.

My mother was a Mexican immigrant, and my father's family emigrated from Italy at the turn of the 20th century. My three brothers and I did not grow up with much money, but we had each other. We grew up in Highland Park, Illinois, with access to a first-rate education. And while there was much to be grateful for, our childhood also taught us about the pain of being different. My mother, brilliant and beautiful, started college at 14 in Mexico. She wanted to be a doctor, but when she arrived to this country, she was bullied and mocked for how she looked and spoke.

Our lives changed forever when she died suddenly at age 50 from complications related to diabetes. I was just 16 years old, and in that moment, I had to grow up. I had to reframe my life and redefine my path. My brothers and I did the best we could, building fulfilling personal and professional lives for ourselves. But I have never forgotten the way people showed up with compassion during my darkest days. That experience forever shaped me and will stay with me for the rest of my life. It is why making a difference matters so deeply to me, especially in the areas of mentoring, equity and inclusion.

As my mother's only daughter, I will always carry her dreams with me. I feel a responsibility to achieve what she could not, and to help others believe in themselves and persevere. This is my family's living legacy."

David's Legacy: Justice, Integrity, and Tikkun Olam

"Two of the most influential people in my life are my parents. Though they passed away many years ago, their voices still guide me in everything I do, in how I practice law, mentor, volunteer and champion inclusion initiatives.

My mother was a teacher. She created what became a lab school in Decatur, Illinois, pioneering "spontaneous learning," which focused on honoring each child's unique pace of learning. She considered herself a "professional volunteer" and served on countless boards, and was the first woman president of our synagogue.

My father was a lawyer, a true professional, who practiced with integrity, humility, and compassion. He treated everyone with equal dignity, regardless of race, gender, religion, or socioeconomic status. He believed in fighting for the underdog and standing up for the marginalized. In the 1960s, my father was one of the only white attorneys providing legal services to the Black community in Decatur. As president of the Decatur Bar Association, he secured permanent funding for a legal aid clinic to serve those who had long been excluded from legal representation. Like my mother, he served on multiple civic and nonprofit boards. And like her, he was also president of our synagogue.

I carry their legacy in all that I do. Over the past few decades, I have mentored hundreds of college and law students and served on numerous nonprofit boards. The foundation of my work is the Jewish tradition of Tikkun Olam— literally to repair the world, with our job in life being to leave the world a better place than when we entered it. That is my inheritance and my parents' legacy."

Your Legacy Starts Now

Your legacy is not something you think about only at the end of your career. You build upon it every day through the choices you make, the people you empower, and the values you uphold. Whether it is through your business, your community work, your mentorship or your personal relationships, how you show up matters. Do not wait for the "right moment" to begin - the time is now. That moment is already here. Make your mark intentionally, courageously and with heart. What you do today is the legacy you leave tomorrow.

Recommended Reading List

- *A Minute to Think*, by Juliet Funt

- *Built to Last*, by Jim Collins & Jerry I. Porras

- *Drive*, by Daniel H. Pink

- *Emotional Intelligence: Why It Can Matter More Than IQ*, by Daniel Goleman

- *Emotional Intelligence 2.0*, by Dr. Travis Bradberry & Dr. Jean Greaves

- *Feel Good Productivity*, by Ali Abdaal

- *Freakonomics*, by Steven D. Levitt & Stephen J. Dubner

- *From Strength to Strength*, by Arthur C. Brooks

- *Good to Great*, by Jim Collins

- *Leading in the Law with Emotional Intelligence: The Path to Becoming a Twenty-First-Century* **Leader**, by Rob Durr & Cliff Zimmerman

- *Memories, Dreams, Reflections*, by Carl Jung

- *Mirroring People*, by Marco Iacoboni

- *Moneyball*, by Michael Lewis

- *My Beloved World*, by Sonia Sotomayor

- *Outliers*, by Malcolm Gladwell

- *Quiet: The Power of Introverts in a World That Can't Stop Talking*, by Susan Cain

- *Revenge of the Tipping Point*, by Malcolm Gladwell

- *Start with Why*, by Simon Sinek

- *Steve Jobs*, by Walter Isaacson

- *Strategy and the Fat Smoker: Doing What's Obvious but Not Easy*, by David Maister

- *Super Freakonomics*, by Steven D. Levitt & Stephen J. Dubner

- *The Greatest Business Decisions of All Time*, by Verne Harnish

- *The Speed of Trust*, by Stephen M.R. Covey

- *The Tipping Point*, by Malcolm Gladwell

- *Where Good Ideas Come From: The Natural History of Innovation*, by Steven Johnson

Additional Resources

Be sure to check out the **Paradigm Shift Podcast** by scanning the QR code below or by searching on your favorite podcast streaming platform.

We welcome any thoughts, questions and feedback you may have regarding this or any of the other titles in the *Paradigm Shift Series.* Our contact information is available below. We would love to hear from you!

Christina L. Martini
christinamartini.paradigmshift@gmail.com

David G. Susler
davidsusler.paradigmshift@gmail.com

NOTES

NOTES

NOTES

NOTES

Notes

NOTES

NOTES

NOTES

Notes

Notes

Notes

Notes

NOTES

NOTES

NOTES

NOTES

NOTES

Notes

NOTES

Notes

NOTES

Notes

NOTES

NOTES

www.ingramcontent.com/pod-product-compliance
Lightning Source LLC
Jackson TN
JSHW042126110825
89192JS00019B/137